BIRDS
DO IT, TOO

BIRDS DO IT, TOO

Text by
KIT HARRISON

Edit and Art Direction by
GEORGE HARRISON

Paintings by
MICHAEL JAMES RIDDET

WILLOW CREEK PRESS

Published in 1997
by Willow Creek Press
P.O. Box 147
Minocqua, WI 54548

For information on other Willow Creek Press titles, call 1-800-850-WILD

**Library of Congress
Cataloging-in-Publication Data**
Harrison, Kit.
    Birds do it, too / text by Kit Harrison ; edit and art direction by George Harrison : paintings by Michael James Riddet.
        p.   cm.
    Includes bibliographical references (p.).
    ISBN 1-57223-092-4 (alk. paper)
    1. Birds--Behavior. 2. Sexual behavior in animals. I. Harrison, George, H. II. Title.
QL698.3.H37 1997
598.156'2--dc21   97-22451
                                                                          CIP

Printed in the United States of America

TABLE OF CONTENTS

ILLUSTRATIONS

ACKNOWLEDGMENTS

We are grateful to the literally hundreds of researchers worldwide whose work has given us an intimate look at the sex lives of the birds. Although we've been fortunate in having been able to observe for ourselves many of the behaviors described in this book, we've also relied on personal observations reported by the scientists studying particular species.

When we started to delve into the masses of technical literature, Dr. Linda Birch, Librarian of the Alexander Library at Oxford University in England, eased our way and minimized our frustration. She was extraordinarily patient with our requests and questions, rarely blushing despite the subject matter, and had a remarkable knowledge of the items in the library. Our days there were idyllic. Thank you, Dr. Birch.

Thanks, too, to Dr. Stanley A. Temple, Beers-Bascom Professor in Conservation in the Department of Wildlife Ecology at the University of Wisconsin–Madison, who provided access to the university's excellent ornithology and biology libraries and also read the manuscript for us.

Joyce Dettmers read the manuscript, too, for clarity, and we are grateful for all her constructive comments and constant encouragement.

Dr. Randall Dettmers, University of Tennessee, was always willing to double-check a reference for us, and to do it promptly and in his usual good-natured way.

Among many others who provided motivation and support were Hal and Mada Harrison, Jack and Jill Hazlett, Jack and Mary Ann Brendel, and Edee Greene, who expressed unwavering confidence in this project.

We are especially grateful to Michael James Riddet, whose paintings enrich this book. He worked long days, often well into the night, to be certain that he depicted every bird and every situation correctly, both anatomically and behaviorally. Thanks, Mike. You've been a delight.

INTRODUCTION

Birds Do It, Too has been incubating for more than 15 years, a time in which we watched in fascination as the study of behavioral ecology progressed with astonishing speed.

An explosion in the number of researchers spending entire seasons in the field, combined with phenomenal technological advancements, turbo-charged the amassing of knowledge.

Now, each new issue of the various scientific journals seems to introduce new discoveries about birds' sexual relationships or behavior, as well as documentation of long-held but never-proven theories about them.

When DNA fingerprinting techniques were added to the tool kits of field ornithologists in the late 1980s, it produced shocking discoveries about some species that we had been led to believe were paragons of monogamy and fidelity.

Our nephew, Dr. Randall Dettmers, an ornithologist at the University of Tennessee, casually mentioned to us one day that DNA fingerprinting had exposed rampant adultery in the hooded warbler nests he had surveyed in southern Ohio. He also told us about the work of Dr. Bridget Stutchbury, who conducted and published research revealing even higher rates of hooded warbler infidelity. Dr. Stutchbury found that around 45 percent of the females had been unfaithful, which resulted in about 30 percent of the nestlings being illegitimate.

What was going on? A lot of extra-marital fooling around by both males and females, that's what. And not just by hooded warblers. It may have been this, more than anything, that convinced us it was time to hatch *Birds Do It, Too*.

We pored through stacks of books, journals, theses, and reprints in the ornithological library of the Edward Gray Institute at Oxford University in England, and continued our research in America, especially at the biology and wildlife ecology libraries of the University of Wisconsin-Madison.

We had known about bird lesbians, prostitutes, hen-pecked husbands, ménage à trois relationships, harems of both males and females, and getting foster parents to raise unwanted children. By the time we had finished, we also found masturbation, pedophilia, necrophilia, and sex changes, to name a few. In short, there is nearly every form of aberrant sexual behavior in birds that there is in people.

Of course, it is important to refrain from judging birds and other animals by our own moral values. They aren't immoral, after all, merely amoral. Their strongest drive is to reproduce, and they'll use whatever system best accomplishes that goal.

In addition, scientists always cringe at the use of anthropomorphism, (attributing human characteristics to animals), and both of us have behaved ourselves pretty well in that regard in what we've written over the years. But this subject seemed to scream for blatant anthropomorphism, and maybe a pinch of light-hearted morality, too, so for once we're defying convention to have a bit of fun.

As bizarre and incredulous as some of the situations in this book may seem, all are based on documentation and observations by dedicated scientists. In other words, all of these scenarios occur. Generally, they are based on relatively new findings, as the bibliography reflects. With a few exceptions, the technical literature from which we gleaned these gems was published in the 1980s and 1990s.

We'll begin with some sweetly romantic gestures and then get into the racier bits. Proceed at your own risk. Some of the material may be X-rated.

HOW BIRDS DO IT

In most songbirds, it is the female that selects a mate. An American robin female may be drawn to a particular male by his song, one of the most effective tools he employs to attract an available female and to advertise possession of his territory to rivals.

BOY MEETS GIRL: THE MATING GAME

With each spring day, the male American robin was feeling increasingly macho, not to mention intensely horny. At the same time, he was finding that the sight of any other robin in the territory he had staked out was extremely agitating to him . . . downright intolerable, actually. Assuming that each was a competitor trying to usurp what was his, he would confront the dastardly scoundrel, flying at him in a fierce kamikaze-style attack that inevitably sent the interloper packing.

Then, one golden morning in early March, he was about to take out his fury on yet another intruder that he had spotted in the fence row, but stopped short. Whoa! This stranger was somewhat paler than he, and clearly no competitor. It was an unattached female that had heard him singing and stopped in to take a closer look at his fine territory . . . and at him. It was an electrifying moment.

Puffing out his chest, he lifted his head and serenaded her with an exuberant rendition of his favorite aria, *Cheer-up! Cheer-up!* She was duly impressed, so after just a few coy maneuvers to maintain a respectable distance between them, she allowed him to approach her. It was almost love at first sight, and after a whirlwind courtship, they knew they were perfect for one another. By the end of the day, they were nearly inseparable and their hormones were raging. By the next morning, they were honeymooning.

Spring in the temperate zones of the world brings more to life than the daffodils and forsythia. The sex organs of birds are also blooming in the year-round residents as well as in the migratory birds that have spent the winter in more sensible climates.

Typically, the mating game is similar to the one most people play — boy meets girl, they court, become husband and wife, furnish a nursery, and raise a family.

In a traditional pairing of songbirds, like robins, cardinals, finches, warblers and wrens, the male establishes occupancy on a site that he believes will provide adequate food, protection, and nesting sites for his bride and their family. That done, he patrols the imaginary borders of his personal habitat with machismo maneuvers, battling any trespassing rivals.

He joins the dawn chorus every morning to proclaim his holdings, and also, it is now believed, to boast to any females within earshot. It's his way of advertising that he is so robust he can delay breakfast and start the day with glorious song instead.

If the male and female have been in residence together throughout the winter, as with cardinals, chickadees and jays, they will probably already be paired. In migratory birds, like orioles, warblers and wrens, the male and female of the species usually return to the breeding grounds separately, the male generally arriving first to claim his territory. When a migratory female arrives from the sunny south, she shops around until she happens upon both a male and a territory that sets her aflutter.

In most cases, it is the bride who selects the groom, so the titillated male does all he can to persuade the lady that he is the man of her dreams. He will now add to his serenade a bit of posturing, bowing, feather fluffing, swaying, or some other display of male braggadocio, depending on his species, to impress the new girl in the neighborhood. As likely as not, she'll appear indifferent, or may reject him outright by fleeing before he comes on too strong.

If she is enthralled, however, she'll eventually discard her demure conduct, and offer herself in a way that leaves him no doubt she's as hot for him as he is for her. Sex, and plenty of it, seems inevitable.

But how, exactly, do birds *do it*?

Even people who are enthusiastic bird watchers often have only a vague idea of how birds have sex. Perhaps some of them don't really want to read such smut about their feathered fancies. For the rest, though, here's a brief biology lesson.

Barn swallows demonstrate what few people understand: how birds do it.

THE EQUIPMENT

Birds, unlike mammals, have no external sex organs, which may be why they seem so pure and innocent to some people. Don't be fooled. They simply keep their mysterious sexual apparatus tucked away in a very compact form until it's needed.

Male birds have two testes, nestled on the lower wall of the abdomen under the small of the back. From each testis, a tube, the *vas deferens,* or sperm duct, opens into the cloaca.

Female birds have two ovaries, yet in almost all species, only the left one is functional; the right one remains undeveloped. From the left ovary, eggs pass through a tube called the oviduct to the cloaca.

Those body parts, in both the male and the female, should be familiar to all of us, until we get to that cloaca thing. The cloaca is an all-purpose passage through which a bird expels urine and feces, as well as sperm from males and eggs from females. The opening of the cloaca is the vent.

Strange as it may seem to mammals like us, male birds of most species manage to engage in sex without having a penis. Such an appendage is rare in birds, though not unknown. Cassowaries, emus, kiwis, ostriches and waterfowl have them. In the ostrich, the retractable phallus is nearly 8 inches long. Waterfowl, like ducks, geese and swans, have a retractable, grooved, almost corkscrew penis which helps guide sperm into the female. (Is this the derivation of the term "screwing"?)

Birds undergo dramatic physiological changes internally when they come into breeding condition. These modifications are brought on primarily by high doses of hormones produced by the pituitary gland at the base of the brain. This rouses the gonads to action (ovaries and testes) which, in turn, produce their own hormones. In the tropics, the onset of the rainy season may trigger this. In temperate zones, the lengthening of daylight in spring provides the stimulus.

Amazing things start to happen. For example, a male's testes may grow to 500 times their off-season size and weigh up to 400 times more, sometimes comprising 10 percent of the bird's body mass. The female's ovaries and oviduct also balloon.

In both sexes, the cloaca bulges into external lips. Don't expect to be able to pick up your binocular and check this out. Normally, you won't see the swollen cloaca of the robin building its nest in your garden unless you are holding the bird in your hand and deliberately trying to get a peek at its private parts. The bird's ventral feathers discreetly cover this area.

... AND HOW IT'S USED

To make baby birds, the male and female must connect their cloacas in order for sperm to be transferred from the male into the female. This is when it gets a little awkward, at least from our perspective, because the cloacas are situated under the tail, at the bottom of the abdomen. If all birds did it face-to-face (like the stitchbirds in New Zealand sometimes do), it might work better, but they don't. Still, it's no problem. The male mounts the female from the rear, she moves her tail out of the way and twists her abdomen sideways, he curves his tail and abdomen downward, and they both invert their cloacas to achieve copulation, or what is often referred to as the cloacal kiss.

THE RECORD HOLDERS

The sex act itself is usually quite brief, sometimes so fleeting that it's hard to believe sperm was actually transferred. For some birds, cloacal contact may last less than a second.

Others, it seems, don't want it to end. One pair of fiery-throated hummingbirds was observed in a cloacal clench for at least 50 minutes, and may actually have been at it much longer. A pair of vasa parrots, one of the species in which the male has a penis-like organ, typically locked their cloacas together for 100 minutes or more.

Skylarks have sex only once to produce a clutch of eggs, yet one successful insemination is indeed enough to fertilize an entire clutch. However, the skylark's puritanical attitude toward sex (one carnal episode per year) is highly unusual; most birds have a healthy interest in sex and go at it frequently during their fertile period. Northern goshawks are probably the record holders in this category; they've been known to make love 600 times for a single clutch of three to four eggs.

Once the sperm enters the female's cloaca, it works its way up her oviduct over the next two or three days to fertilize the egg that has been released from her ovary. The egg is laid 24 hours after it has been fertilized. Most female birds lay an egg a day until the clutch is complete, though in a few species, it may be every two to three days.

The reason that one insemination can fertilize an entire clutch, even though there is only one egg in the oviduct at a time, is that female birds can store sperm for at least a week, and occasionally as long as a month. Some female seabirds are able to store viable sperm for 72 days, the domestic turkey for 117 days. We are far less proficient at this than the birds. A woman can retain sperm that is capable of fertilization for a maximum of only 48 hours.

THEME AND VARIATIONS

Most songbirds are monogamous, and enter into a temporary marriage that lasts through one breeding season. (Avian monogamy, however, should not be confused with fidelity.) Other birds might be bigamists or polygamists. When the male is a polygamist, like the ring-necked pheasant, it's called polygyny. When the female has two or more husbands, as in the spotted sandpiper, it's polyandry. Some birds like to mix it up with a mating system called polygynandry, in which both males and females have multiple husbands or lovers.

A few species, especially those in which the offspring require little or no parental care, are entirely promiscuous. There is no marriage. The male and female come together only for the purpose of a sexual encounter, the avian version of a one-night stand. The female handles all domestic and family duties – building the nest, incubating the eggs and rearing the young. The only contribution the male makes to the female is his sperm. . . . although, in many cases, he also provides some jolly good entertainment. Birds of paradise, certain sandpipers, some grouse, a few hummingbirds, and the cock-of-the-rock expend enormous amounts of energy making fools of themselves in their endeavors to show off to the ladies.

Within this complexity of mating systems is almost every sort of relationship, normal and abnormal, that is found in humans, although we haven't found any blatant examples of sado-masochism in birds . . . at least, not yet. There are, however, many hen-pecked husbands. It's not unusual for the female of a pair to become dominant over her husband, especially once the nesting cycle has begun. He becomes more solicitous to her, she becomes more impatient and demanding with him.

When a pair is renesting, either to produce a second brood or because their first nest was destroyed, the male might lag behind in his readiness to breed again. If so, the female in some species may take the situation in hand by mounting him. Other times, reverse mounting may simply be part of their courtship.

Sometimes a hen-pecked male chaffinch is so intimidated by his wife that he approaches her with great trepidation, timidly pussy-footing toward her, a few steps at a time, and then retreating again. Eventually, following a hesitant, zig-zagging route, Mr. Peepers draws to within several inches of Brunhilda, struggling to control his throaty rattles of terror, especially if she turns and threatens him with an open bill. If he is able to overcome the conflict between his fear of attack and his desire for her, he'll hover nervously above his lady love and gently settle down onto her back. If she's in a good mood, she won't start pecking him while he's trying to make love to her.

The male willet, a long-legged wader, might be subjected to the shocking experience of having his wife, during an intimate moment, toss him forward over her shoulders into the shallow water at her feet. Oh, the indignity of it all. Undeterred, he usually goes back for more.

Some males turn their affections to sweet young things, literally robbing the cradle. Would-be pedophiles have been reported in species as diverse as wren-tits and pectoral sandpipers (which will court almost anything). In the case of the wren-tit, it may have been a response to the fledgling wren-tit's begging posture, which is similar to a female's solicitation for sex — crouched, with fluttering wings.

However, unpaired adult male Chiloe wigeons have boldly courted female ducklings, some as young as nine days old. When the vivacious ducklings were six to eight weeks old, some of the dirty old men had succeeded in forming pair bonds with them, in spite being aggressively chased by the ducklings' disapproving parents.

Birds seem to draw the line at incest. It is extremely rare, because there are built-in mechanisms to prevent inbreeding. One of the most effective is the voluntary dispersal, or sometimes the forceful booting out, of young birds from the parents' territory. Even among colonial nesters, or species in which the next generation or two hang around to help raise the next batch, it is usually avoided. There are exceptions. Incest is known to occur in the superb blue wren and is common in the pukeko, or swamphen . . . of course, this bird will try almost anything.

I WANT A DIVORCE

As with people, avian marriages don't always work out. Birds are considered divorced when both members of a mated pair are still alive and one or both select a different mate for the next consecutive breeding season. Or, they may divorce and switch mates between nestings within a single season.

Reasons for avian divorce, as for human divorce, are complex. Some of the major factors appear to be desertion, adultery, and, probably more than anything, failure to successfully raise a family.

Those are the basics of bird sex. Now, on to advanced techniques, variations, deviations, aberrations, and debauchery.

COURTSHIP
AND
SEDUCTION

A seemingly tender moment is shared by a pair of courting blue jays. Kissing? In this case, it's more like a dinner date, because he's just passed a sunflower seed to her. Sometimes they touch bills even when no food is passed between them.

THE DINNER DATE

A flash of blue streaks into the century-old oak of a suburban garden and settles on a horizontal branch, still leafless in the earliest days of spring. Almost immediately, another bolt of blue flies in, taking its place beside the first.

They are a pair of blue jays, mated for some time, but still keeping the spark of their relationship alive with little courtship rituals. He now has a sunflower seed in his bill, and charmingly offers it to his mate, who daintily accepts it in her own bill. Unless you look closely, it may appear that they've exchanged a quick kiss, and in fact, sometimes no food is actually passed between them. They may merely touch the tips of their bills in an endearing, symbolic gesture.

Meanwhile, in the Sonoran Desert, a male roadrunner has caught a small lizard and is taking it back to his mate, who just began building a nest that morning. Tail wagging, he approaches her with a low, whirring call, and shows her the lizard he is holding by its neck in his bill. The female, seeing her spouse and the gift he has brought, runs to stand in front of him, tail raised. Still holding the lizard, the male jumps onto her back, and as they share a cloacal kiss, the lizard is transferred from his bill to hers.

High above a distant marsh, a male harrier has been calling his shrill scream for several minutes. He has a vole in his talons, a token for his lady, and is trying to entice her to rendezvous with him. At last she appears, flying up to join him. When she is about 15 feet beneath him, he releases the vole. She gracefully turns over, almost on her back, stretches out her feet, and deftly catches the vole in her talons.

Most men know that providing dinner for a date, or even for a spouse of many years, could be just what is needed to spark the romantic fire that he has been trying to ignite in her.

It's much the same in many birds. Feeding is an important part of courtship and family life for a number of species. It is most often found in monogamous birds, especially those in which the male participates in feeding his offspring.

It may give a female an indication of whether a prospective suitor will be a good provider for her and her young, and the extra nutrition can translate into heavier clutches of eggs and better survival for chicks. In some cases, the male uses it as an enticement for sex. For example, in roadrunners, food is involved in about 75 percent of their lovemaking.

More than anything, though, courtship feeding serves to strengthen pair bonds. For some, it begins in the early stages of their relationship and continues until the young have fledged. In others, it is more properly termed nuptial feeding, because food is provided at the nest, after marriage, to feed the incubating mate and, later, the chicks.

Most bird watchers have seen at least one instance of courtship feeding, often right outside their windows. In America, you may catch a northern cardinal or blue jay on a bird feeder passing a seed to its mate. At a British bird table, a male European robin might feed his lady.

Typically, the male feeds the female, but sometimes they feed each other. In a few of the role-reversed species, in which the female does the courting and the male assumes incubation chores, she may feed him.

With rhythmic booms and dazzling footwork, male prairie chickens try to outdo one another in their eagerness to impress an audience of hens. The girls may appear to be unimpressed with the dancing skills of these dandies, but looks are deceptive. They're evaluating every move.

SONG AND DANCE MEN

Dawn is still half an hour away, but through the patchy ground fog, small apparitions advance over the dewy grass to a slight rise. Each takes his position on the open-air stage, and goes through a warm-up routine in rehearsal for his dance performance.

Each has a modest clearing on the prairie grass which serves as his dancing stage, the borders invisible, yet clearly defined. The gray sky begins to brighten as the sun, barely peeping over the horizon, provides footlights, casting a golden hue on the performers. In the growing illumination, they no longer resemble miniature phantoms; it is obvious that they are splendid, virile greater prairie chicken males.

The mating season has reached a crescendo for these members of the grouse family, and more than 40 cocks have converged on their ancestral booming ground, or lek, impatiently anticipating the arrival of the hens.

There is no loitering. Every male takes this ritual very seriously, and before long, all are either working hard at perfecting their technique or bullying their subordinate neighbors.

When the hens, smaller and plainer, begin to nonchalantly saunter into the lek, often one or two at a time, the males kick into high gear, each one trying to outdo the other to capture the girls' attention.

With head lowered, the long feathers that normally rest on the back of the male's head and neck are erected to resemble feathered rabbit ears ... or perhaps cupid wings. Eyebrows bulge, looking like fuzzy golden caterpillars resting above the bird's nose, wings droop, and two bright orange air sacs, one on each side of the throat, inflate with air. The fanned tail is raised as high as it will go, and the feet drum a tattoo of love that beats ever faster, until the feet virtually disappear in a blur. He moves like an over-wound toy as he pirouettes to maintain a full-frontal presentation to the closest hen.

The pièce de résistance of the cock's performance, executed periodically, is the boom, the *ah-bah-whoooomp!* produced as air is forcefully expelled from the inflated sacs.

Meanwhile, the girls, giving the exasperating impression of being utterly bored, peck at imaginary seeds or bits of grass on the ground, casually making their way through the entire assemblage to evaluate all the candidates. Their indifference is a ruse; they're registering every nuance.

A hen may visit the dance court two or three times before making her choice, or she may mate with one or more males on each of her visits. Invariably, the honor will go to one of the dominant males whose territory is near the center of the booming ground.

Decision made, she approaches the strutting cock, who responds by spreading his wings and bowing deeply, his chin nearly touching the ground. She draws near, crouches, and in a twinkling, his cloaca is kissing hers.

Successfully bred, the hen leaves the mating arena to scratch out a nest, lay her eggs and raise the chicks on her own.

Back at the booming ground, the show will continue for two or three hours every morning until all breeding females have been fertilized, including any that come back for a second round after having lost a nest.

Prairie chickens are among the species in ten families of birds that use communal areas, called leks, that are reserved expressly for the males' courtship displays and mating. The sage grouse, black grouse, capercaillie, cock-of-the-rock, and ruff are some of the most renowned.

Typically, a few of the males are favored with most of the breeding; others may not win any females. Very often, when one or two females show interest in a particular male, it piques the curiosity of other females and soon a crowd gathers.

The elaborate dancing, strutting, posturing and other ritualized aspects of the performances are not learned, but are innate. Baby male prairie chickens can perform a rendition of their father's dance when they are just a few hours old.

As graceful and athletic as ballet dancers, sandhill crane pairs engage in an elegant pas de deux when courting, and sometimes at other times, too, apparently simply for the sheer enjoyment of dancing.

PAS DE DEUX

In a boggy meadow in south-central Nebraska, an early morning performance is about to begin, a graceful yet high-spirited ballet danced by a pair of sandhill cranes.

The stately four-foot-tall gray birds first bow slowly and deeply to one another before warming up with a couple of pliés. Then, facing each other, they take turns springing into the air, low bounces at first, but eventually rising more than six feet off the ground. Sometimes, both birds are aloft at the same time. Now and then, one may execute a grand jeté, leaping high over the head of its mate and landing on the other side. Red-crowned heads bob, wings flap, and occasionally one picks up a twig and flings it overhead. It can only be interpreted as a dance of jubilation on this fine mid-March morning.

Their exuberance is contagious, and before long, other couples and small groups pause in their feeding to perform their own dances.

The pair that initiated the frolic eventually stop as quickly as they began. Standing tall, they raise their voices in short, loud, triumphant bugles, each trumpet alternating between the male and female.

Finally, they begin to feed quietly, in perfect harmony, the head of one always up when the other is down, their statuesque elegance restored.

In another week or two, they will leave their ancestral staging area along the Platte River. They have congregated there with half a million others of their kind, resting and building up body weight before flying on to marshes and bogs farther north where each pair will claim a territory and raise a chick or two.

Although it was spring, it could have been any season. Cranes just seem to enjoy dancing for the sake of dance. Cranes of all species dance, regardless of age or sex, any time of the year, and for various reasons, although it is performed most often between pairs during courtship.

Even baby cranes dance when they're merely a few days old, a performance that seems generated from nothing more than sheer joy of life.

Another couples dance, quite spectacular, is the water ballet of some of the grebes. Western grebes, striking black and white birds with gleaming red eyes, begin with an allegro movement. They approach each other and rise up, wings lifted and long necks extended forward, to begin an upright rush across the surface of the water. Running side-by-side, they pick up speed, their feet churning so fast under them that they seem to be propelled by inboard Mercuries.

At the end of the mad dash, the male dives beneath the surface, immediately followed by the female. They emerge, reestablish contact with one another, and may then opt to proceed to the weed dance, their adagio segment. Diving first, each bird surfaces with a bill full of the type of weeds they will use in their nest construction. They glide toward each other and push with their feet to raise themselves into a face-to-face, almost vertical posture. Bills stretched upward, they bring them together to join the weeds, a gesture that is elegant but meaningful, signifying a pair bond.

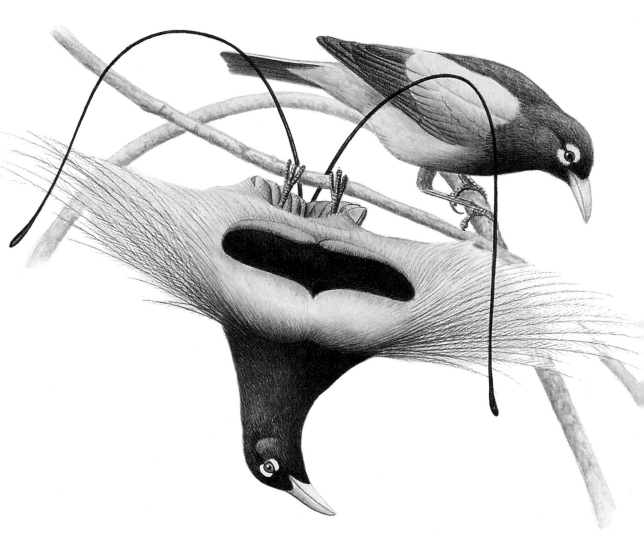

Some guys will fall head over heels for a girl. Even at that, the spectacular male blue bird of paradise will have to work hard to woo her. She'll expect him to really flip for her — and he will, since it's the best way to show off his elaborate plumage.

HUNKS

There are times when a girl may be drawn irresistibly to a dazzling Casanova, even though she knows that the most she can expect from him is a one-night stand. She's thrilled. He's the most gorgeous thing she's ever seen, and he's doing everything he can to impress her. She tries to appear indifferent; she doesn't want to be seen as a lady of easy virtue. Still, she's taken a look at the other guys that were putting the moves on her, and she knows that this dandy is the one for her. He exudes grace, his finery is unparalleled, and he knows how to flaunt it. And, obviously, he's fallen head over heels for her.

She — a female blue bird of paradise — is visiting the display area of an available male, lured by the sound of his voice, a bit hoarse, yet pleasant to her ears. Once she appears, he swings into action, literally. Singing from his horizontal perch, he begins his elaborate performance by bending forward, farther and farther, until he is hanging completely upside down. Captivated, she watches from above as he spreads a spectacular profusion of long, frilly, ornamental plumes in lavish, iridescent blues and violets. Then, swinging rhythmically back and forth by his toes, he quivers his remarkable feathers to display them to even greater advantage. The female is smitten.

They breed right there on his perch, then she slips away, alone, into the rain forest to lay her eggs, incubate them, and raise the youngsters entirely on her own.

Meanwhile, the father of her babies is still hanging out in the same spot, seducing any female that he can beguile with his charms.

There are 43 known bird of paradise species, 36 of them in New Guinea, the rest in Australia and Indonesia. Nearly all are polygynous or promiscuous. Of these, each species has unique plumage which the male displays to its full advantage through various types of acrobatics, dances or poses.

Birds of paradise are the among most spectacular of the birds that attract females with exaggerated ornamentation. The peacock is another. It is easily bred in captivity and is often a living decoration on large estates or in public gardens, where it is easy to observe.

Here, the male strolls through the grounds trailing his elaborate train, which is not his tail but elongated feathers on his back. In the presence of a peahen during the breeding season, the peacock raises these feathers and spreads them into an enormous fan, curving it forward toward the female. The iridescent blues, greens, violets and golds create a dramatic pattern that looks like dozens of eyes. From time to time, the peacock vibrates his fan, creating an audible rustle among the feathers. At some point, he turns around to display himself from the back. The view from this angle is not nearly as appealing to our own sense of aesthetics, but the hen takes it all in stride, and before long, he again turns to reveal the jewel-like splendor of his feather fan.

Another bird that has a special adaptation for getting the attention of potential mates is the magnificent frigatebird. For most of the year, the glossy black male has a thin strip of pinkish skin on his throat. When it's time to court, that strip is transformed into an inflatable red pouch.

In a colony with other males, the frigatebird builds a loose nest of sticks. There he sits, on the empty nest, waiting for a white-chested female to sail over. When one does, he thrusts out the red throat pouch, which he has pumped up with air until it looks as though it will burst, starts his odd, rattling call, sways his head and flutters his wings. When inflated, the scarlet sac, called a gular pouch, gives the impression that the bird has pinned a huge, heart-shaped, red satin pillow on his breast. If he looks better to the passing female than his competitors, all of whom are putting on the same frenzied presentation, she may settle down on his nest to raise a chick with him.

No one is really certain why some birds have evolved these adornments. Some believe that it came about as a matter of female choice. The birds chosen by females for mating passed along their genes, thereby continuing the trait. Some think that it is a way for males to establish their dominance among other males whose ornamentation may not be as flamboyant. In addition, these appendages create a burden for the male, making it more difficult for him to fly with speed and maneuverability. That would put his survivability at stake. Some say the fact that the bird is, in essence, somewhat handicapped and still manages to survive in spite of it, makes him a desirable mate. The answer may be that all three factors have influenced the development of these embellishments, to a greater or lesser extent, depending on the species. Time will tell; the researchers and behaviorists are still trying to sort it out.

No red-blooded male alpine accentor is going to pass up an invitation like this. The lusty female easily seduces him by getting in front of him and lifting her tail to give him a good look at what she's offering.

SUPER STUDS AND BAWDY BROADS

I t's not how big it is, it's how you use it. At least that's what guys like to tell their partners if they have been a little short-changed in terms of sexual endowment. Dr. Ruth and other sex therapists agree that bigger is not necessarily better, although you'll never convince the alpine accentor, a songbird found in high mountains from Europe to Asia.

Like almost all birds, the male alpine accentor has no penis, but his testes make up 7.7 percent of his body mass during the breeding season. That would be equivalent to a 170-pound human male having over 13 pounds of testicles dangling between his legs, instead of the four ounces or less that he actually has. At the same time, the male accentor's cloaca swells into a distended, bulbous protuberance.

Fortunately for the male, the female of his species is also equipped with exaggerated sex organs during her fertile period, and seems to be even more lusty than he. Inevitably, it is she who initiates sex. She's an exhibitionist, doing her own interpretation of a seductress raising her skirt and murmuring, "I'm not wearing any panties . . . wanna see?" She approaches one or more males, turns around, bends over, and lifts her tail to expose her own pulsing, scarlet protrusion.

Seeing this, the male needs no further prodding; he mounts her immediately. But, as soon as he's finished, she wants more. She may flash the same male again to prompt another quickie, or she might expose herself to others, perhaps mating with three different males, one after the other, in less than three minutes. By the end of the day, she might have solicited 30 copulations. By the end of her fertile period, she is likely to have had sex with every male in her social group . . . and each male will probably have had sex with every female.

Unusually large cloacal protuberances are found in bird species in which males face intense sperm competition, as do the alpine accentors. Every male wants to be the father of each female's babies. The testes are greatly enlarged in the male, and the swelling of the seminal glomera (sperm store) creates the cloacal protrusion. A few other birds in which the males develop extremely exaggerated cloacas are the dunnock, Smith's longspur, superb and splendid fairy-wrens, and aquatic warblers.

Apparently the oversized testes and sperm stores are necessary to maintain the high copulation rates and produce the large amounts of sperm required in the pursuit of paternity assurance. The Smith's longspur, for example, usually copulates about 365 times per clutch, although one female was observed going at it 629 times. Taking into consideration that the birds only copulate over a span of about 6 ½days, the hourly rate is mind-boggling. With that kind of pressure to perform, it's no wonder the males have developed impressive equipment to enable them to rise to the task.

Competition between males within a breeding group, and instances of females sneaking sex outside the group, are so rife in splendid and superb fairy-wrens that about 80 percent of all offspring are sired by males other than those within the breeding group, the highest recorded for any bird species. That type of intense competition is probably why the male's testes comprise 10 percent of his body weight during the breeding season.

Another interesting feature of the male superb fairy-wren is that it has a cartilaginous tip on the cloacal protuberance, and may be inserted into the female's cloaca during copulation, like a penis, to more effectively transfer sperm.

Love is in the air. White-throated swifts make love on the wing, throwing caution to the wind as they plummet towards the earth.

THRILL SEEKERS: THE MILE-HIGH CLUB

Have you ever had sex onboard a soaring airplane?   If so, you're a member of the Mile High Club.   On a commercial flight, a pair of horny passengers might be talented and acrobatic enough to sneak into one of the lavatories in the tail, one at a time, and pull off a surreptitious tryst.   Some young men and women have taken private planes high into the air and left the controls unmanned while they joined the club.   Tragically, some of these crash landed, and the occupants never got to flaunt passing their initiation.

Well, some birds do it, too.   Take the pair of white-throated swifts that Dr. Stanley Temple observed one day in southern Colorado.   The two birds became one, right in midair, and, in their apparent rapture, didn't seem to notice that they were forgetting to fly.   They dropped several hundred feet, pinwheeling as they fell, and crash landed on top of a cliff close to Temple's observation point, where they lay motionless, still entwined.   Lo and behold, a few minutes later, they began to stir.   It's not hard to imagine one chippering to the other, "Gee, honey, I saw stars that time!"

White-throated swifts spend most of their lives on the wing, and typically copulate in midair — but they usually escape crash landings like the one Stan Temple saw.

Many birds have aerial courtship displays, from the enchanting, twittering hover flights of larks and bobolinks and the deep undulating U flights of hummingbirds, to the swoops and backward somersaults of the scissor-tailed flycatcher's sky dance, the spiraling and zigzagging of the woodcock, and the dramatic high-speed dives of many members of the hawk family.

Most of these display flights are performed only by the male, but both members of a pair in some species, especially hawks and eagles, may engage in mutual aerial courtship, stopping short of actually having sex on the wing. Of these, perhaps the most breathtaking is executed on some occasions by bald and golden eagles. The male soars up to a height much greater than that at which his mate is flying, then partly folds his wings and dive bombs straight for her, legs dangling. Sometimes he seems to actually tap her on the back with his talons in the instant before swooping upward again. Every now and then, she flips over onto her back at the last second with her own feet extended. The male and female grasp each other's talons and fall earthward, tumbling over and over. Just when it seems certain they are going to smash full-speed into the earth, they break off and surge skyward again.

These birds, like some people, may find that danger is a thrill, a real turn-on!

The pendulous, bobbing breast sac of the male pectoral sandpiper is an important asset in his energetic antics to capture the attention of a prospective female.

LIBIDOS IN OVERDRIVE

The pectoral sandpiper must certainly have one of the highest sex drives of all birds. Understandable, perhaps, when you consider the circumstances. He must squeeze a whole year's worth of promiscuous sex into the span of a few weeks.

He flies from South America to the arctic tundra, arriving in late May or early June, for the express purpose of seducing as many females as he possibly can. After that, he hightails south again, leaving the consequences of his promiscuity to the females that he has inseminated.

During the brief breeding season, the male's otherwise imperceptible breast sac becomes a pendulous, low-hanging, matronly bosom. There's nothing matronly, though, about his behavior. The pectoral sac is actually an important part of this Lothario's courtship display flight, as he pumps it up and down while hooting his love song. It's a sight the female pectorals can hardly miss, because there's nothing in the tundra landscape to obstruct their view.

When a female is spotted, the playboy launches into a courtship flight, hooting and swooping just over her head and then rising slightly as he flutters and soars in a broad circle, breast sac swinging all the while, but no longer hooting once he is past her.

Upon landing, he runs to her, calling in guttural tones. After catching his aerial shenanigans, the fair damsel may not stay to see what other tricks he has in store, but if she does, he approaches her from the rear with breast sac bobbing. If she's still interested at this point, he becomes so excited that his incessant vocalizations are now wheezes. Finally, he mounts her to share a licentious moment of bliss.

Satisfaction is short-lived, however. As soon as another wench is in sight, he's hankering to do it all over again.

Male pectorals are so horny that they'll court nearly anything that moves, and some things that don't move. If it even remotely resembles a female of their species, it is pursued, which makes it rather dicey for females of other sandpiper species to venture too close.

Male pectoral sandpipers are irredeemable lechers. One stooped to a fleeting but unrewarding stint as a pedophile, trying to court an unfledged dunlin chick, and another resorted to necrophilia, trying to copulate with a dead red phalarope.

Perhaps the height of buffoonery (from a human viewpoint, certainly not theirs) can be found in the buff-breasted sandpiper, another tundra-nesting species. The males gather on leks to attract females. The biggest turn-on for the females seems to be males exposing their underwings.

Picture, if you will, a male buff-breasted, posing proudly on his piece of the lek, head thrown back and wings outstretched. Around him, a small group of females has gathered, each indicating intense interest in every aspect of his wing linings, examining them microscopically. To us, it may look like they're sniffing his armpits, but no, this is serious business to all concerned.

If they like what they see, the girls will present themselves for copulation. Or, they may take their leave as he stands there, still holding his stiff pose. One can almost imagine them sniggering mischievously among themselves, like naughty schoolgirls, as they go off to tease the next male on their list.

That's not the worst indignity that he may have to suffer, however. That happens when, just as everything seems to be going beautifully, and the females look like they're nearly ready to give themselves to him, another male abruptly crashes the party, jumps onto the displaying male's back and tries to copulate. Well, you can understand how that would shatter the mood. The spoiler then beats a quick retreat to his own territory, often trailed by the females that were just beginning to feel amorous.

You have to wonder if some of the males aren't relieved when the breeding season draws to a close so they can regain their dignity.

It's hard to see what male cowbirds find so irresistible about the plain gray females that may have a string of suitors vying for her attentions. She's a party girl with low morals, abandoning her children to the mercy of unsuspecting foster parents.

THE LADY IS A TRAMP

Wanton Sex! Murder! Deception! Homeless infants left to the mercy of unwitting strangers! Blurbs for a steamy new Sydney Sheldon novel? No, just the everyday pastimes of the female cowbird during the breeding season.

She may be seen as a shameless hussy or a liberated woman, reviled or admired, depending on your point of view, but she has figured out how to party, party, party, without having to pay the consequences of promiscuous sex. The early ornithologists must have seen her for what she was, for the name they gave her, *Molothrus,* means tramp.

Little does it matter to the guys that she's a trollop. They adore her. She has an entourage of perhaps half a dozen admirers that nearly fall over themselves as they bow low in homage to her. (Actually, they sometimes *do* topple onto their heads.) While bowing, they spread their wings, show off their glossy cape with a ruffled flourish, and croon a gurgling love song to her. In general, they make a spectacle of themselves in their frenzy to win her favor.

Most often, the ardent paramours try to court her when she's on the go. Flying alongside her, they do their darnedest to show off their feathers and even take a bow in midair, purring intimately to her in guttural tones. Yes, guttural. She's the sort that probably likes it when they talk dirty.

In the air, she plays the coquette, staying just a wingbeat ahead of her excited retinue. It's all part of the game. They are her toy boys, and she leads them all on. She may have a favorite to whom she will be faithful, in her fashion, though she is more likely to give herself to several.

Heaven knows what they see in her. The object of their desire is a gray Plain Jane, yet she obviously knows all the right moves to keep her bevy of beaus lusting after her.

She's a loose woman with low morals who can't be inconvenienced with family responsibilities. Nevertheless, she doesn't bother to practice birth control, which in the bird world basically amounts to "just say no." So, she does the next best thing. In essence, she leaves the baby on the doorstep of another. Each time this floozy has to lay an egg, she first removes one from the nest of another species. After committing this murder, she returns to the scene of the crime to surreptitiously deposit her own egg. She gets up very early in the morning to accomplish this deception, typically pulling off the scam before 5 a.m.

This leaves her with no domestic chores like having to build a nest, no long dreary days of solitary incubation waiting for a passel of dependent babies to come into the world, no scrambling to keep hungry little mouths fed. She's got it made.

Having abandoned her offspring to be raised by unsuspecting foster parents, the wanton wench is back to cavorting with the boys again. Party, party, party, with nary a glance backward.

Cowbirds are among the 75 or so species in six families of birds worldwide that practice what is called brood parasitism. They build no nests of their own, instead laying their eggs in the nests of other birds. About 220 species are known to have been parasitized by cowbirds.

A female cowbird may lay as many as 20 to 50 eggs in a season, but usually deposits only one egg per nest. When cowbird chicks hatch, they are often much larger than their nestmates, who may be tiny warblers, sparrows, or flycatchers. By the time the cowbird chick is ready to leave the nest, it may be larger than its foster parents.

European cuckoos also are adept at getting others to rear their young, and the offspring are just as resourceful as their biological parents. As soon as it hatches, the baby cuckoo manages to push any other eggs or chicks out of the nest. This leaves the undiscerning foster parents with an only child, increasing the chick's survivability.

Cowbirds and cuckoos get away with their trickery because they usually lay their eggs in the nests of birds that are not likely to notice an interloper in the clutch. In the case of European cuckoos, females are often able to lay eggs that mimic those of the foster parent in both color and pattern. Female cuckoos may produce eggs that perfectly match those of the reed warbler, for example, or of the pied wagtail or the meadow pipit, which are among the cuckoo's main victims. Typically, she will choose nests of the same species that raised her. However, since cuckoo eggs have been found in the nests of over 100 species, this does not always hold true.

Certain other species are also guilty of brood parasitism when they lay eggs in the nests of their own kind, a practice known as egg dumping. It has long been known to occur among some ducks and geese, but as the study of behavioral ecology has grown, egg dumping has also been documented in other orders of birds.

Female house wrens occasionally sneak into the nest boxes or cavities of other house wrens and add an egg to the clutch when the owners are absent. The same is true of starlings, where egg dumping may occur in a third to nearly a half of the nests. Purple martins apparently suffer egg dumping to a similar extent.

In cliff swallows, a kind of musical eggs game is played, with the female members of a colony laying eggs in each other's nests, to the point that more than a fifth, and perhaps close to half, of the nests may be parasitized. Occasionally an egg is removed from someone else's nest (perhaps before adding one's own), but apparently this isn't a prerequisite. A cliff swallow may quickly lay an egg directly into another nest, or might transfer an egg. To do this, the bird picks up an egg in its bill and carries it from its own nest to another. While the egg dumper is away parasitizing the nest of a nearby resident, her own nest may be receiving an egg from another trespassing female, who can lay it in as little as 15 seconds. Do unto others . . .

In these species, such behavior may be a way for a bird to increase its reproduction, trying to produce more offspring than it can raise in its own nest. It might also be an insurance policy, a strategy for having at least some of the eggs and chicks survive if the nest of the contributing female is destroyed. Among house wrens and some others, the theory is that a fertilized female, ready to lay an egg, may have lost her nest or her mate, or is a floater female — one that has no mate, nest or territory. Finding a nest, she surreptitiously slips in and deposits an egg.

The practice of egg dumping became more apparent with the advent of DNA fingerprinting. All of a sudden, field researchers were finding nests in which the DNA of one or more of the chicks showed that it was not the offspring of either of the supposed parents.

A man's wealth can be a turn-on for some girls, and the male satin bowerbird seems to know how to exploit this. He constructs an elaborate love nest and decorates it with tantalizing material goods to entice available females.

THE LOVE NEST

A series of croaking calls coming from the undergrowth somewhere ahead of her caught the attention of a female satin bowerbird as she foraged in an eastern Australian forest one day. Her interest piqued, she flew toward the sound, and when she had located it, her eyes fell upon a magnificent sight.

There on the forest floor was an intricate work of architecture. Two parallel walls, woven from slender twigs, rose to a height of about 14 inches, and curved toward each other, creating a U shape. Between the walls, which had been painted bluish gray, ran a corridor carpeted with a thick, densely woven mat of grasses and fine twigs. At the front door was an enchanting miniature meadow, decorated with flowers and many wondrous objects, some of them shiny, most of them in her favorite color, blue, but supplemented with a few yellow accent pieces.

Standing there amidst this wealth of riches was the architect himself, clearly delighted that she was taking an interest in his masterpiece and his possessions. In a flutter of excitement, the male bowerbird picked up one treasure after another to show to her. She appeared to be only mildly interested, and on the verge of moving on. "Look at this!" he seemed to call, trying to detain her. "Have you ever seen such a brilliant blue feather? And what about this blue cat's eye marble . . . is it not extraordinary?"

Yes, she might have thought, indeed it is, but I've seen it somewhere before. It was shown to me by a rival of this fellow about three days ago. He stole it!

Instead of disapproving of the stolen article, its rarity thrilled her, as did all the other wealth that he had succeeded in acquiring and then defending against any who might try to steal from him. Intrigued, she drew closer.

Continuing to flutter and dash around, the male spread his tail and then his wings so that they caught rays of sunshine in a way that flattered his lustrous blue-black plumage. He had her full attention now.

Chattering to her constantly, he watched as she gingerly stepped into the arcade that he had been working on painstakingly over a period of months, continuously renovating, remodeling, and improving it.

The male bowerbird's courtship now reached a wild, frenzied pitch. Time and again he picked up objects, only to furiously throw them down. After a while, his passion inflamed, he joined the female, and then mounted her in the shelter of the structure that he had carefully built for just this purpose.

Immediately afterward, his lust quelled, he drove her out. For this house was not a home. He had used it, and its decorations, to successfully seduce her, just as a girl might be seduced by a man who lures her to his opulent mansion. She sees his Rolls Royce and Ferrari parked in the forecourt, and is dazzled as he gives her a guided tour of the house. She gazes wide-eyed at the art treasures and priceless antiques and artifacts . . . including a spectacular diamond tiara that was known to have been stolen from the Winter Palace in St. Petersburg at the beginning of the revolution.

Bowerbirds are close relatives of birds of paradise, although they are not outfitted in the spectacular plumages that adorn most of their cousins. Instead, they seduce with material goods.

The satin bowerbird, about the size of a common grackle, is one of the larger of the 19 bowerbird species found in Australia or New Guinea. Three of them are monogamous species in which the male and female jointly construct a nest and raise their young; they do not build bowers. The other 16 species are promiscuous or polygynous, and build bowers in a variety of styles.

Some, like the satin bowerbird, are avenue builders. They usually build two walls to create the avenue, and then decorate the adjoining area with shells, insect wings, pebbles, fresh flowers, mosses and feathers. If they are close to civilization, they'll scavenge or steal bits of glass, jewelry, pottery, cutlery, small toys, bottle caps and other doodads. One man awoke to find that his glass eye was missing from his bedside table in the morning. It was later found on exhibit at a nearby bower.

Some avenue builders, like the satin bowerbird, like to paint the walls of their bower. Using charcoal, berries and saliva, they use a small, spongy piece of bark as a tool to apply the paint. Bowerbirds that live near people have been known to steal packets of bluing used for laundry and mix the contents with saliva, creating a gaudy blue paint that the birds find especially appealing.

Other bowerbirds are maypole builders. They create large, cone-shaped structures that are built around one or two small trees. The golden bowerbird, which is the smallest of the family, about the size of a meadowlark, actually builds the largest bower, sometimes nine feet tall. The teepee-like designs of the maypole builders typically have a front entrance opening onto a cleared area that has been decorated by the bird, giving the impression of a garden outside the door.

Still other bowerbirds, categorized as stage makers and mat makers, do not build actual bowers.

Young birds are not adept at bower building; they learn their craft over a series of years. A male starts to build well before the females are interested in seeking mates, and spends most of his daylight hours first building and then perfecting his bower. The male is constantly fussing with his creation. If a flower wilts, he replaces it with a fresh one. He is obsessive about the old adage, "a place for everything, and everything in its place." Researchers who have moved items, or turned them upside down, or faced them in a different direction during the bird's absence found that the owner would invariably move each item back to its original position, no matter how many times it was displaced.

If the opportunity arises, a male bowerbird will plunder a rival's bower when the owner is not in attendance, tearing down some of the structure or making off with a bit of loot, or both.

After mating, the female leaves the bower, often forcibly evicted by the male. She goes off to build a nest, lay the eggs that he fertilized, and raise the young, all on her own.

As soon as she's gone, the male's attention turns once again to his pride and joy. She might be the only female that he'll successfully mate with this season, but another could come along at any time. So, he meticulously repairs any part of the structure that may have been damaged during the sexual escapade, and fusses with each detail until it is once again perfection in his eyes. If a new item is added, he steps back to look at it this way and that, tilting his head with a discerning eye. If it doesn't meet with his approval in that spot, he'll try it in others until he is satisfied.

If he is an experienced male who has built a bower of splendor, he is likely to attract and mate with many females during the breeding season. Yet, even after all the females are busy with nesting chores, indeed even after the young have fledged, the compulsive architect will still be found obsessively tending to his bower. It seems to please him to do so.

I'M GOING TO HAVE YOUR BABY: MARRIAGE ENTRAPMENT

Peering at the six pale blue-green eggs in her nesting cavity, the female pied flycatcher realized that she now had a full clutch and it was time to start incubating. She was in trouble.

Sadly, her mate had been killed yesterday afternoon by a cat whose irresponsible owners allowed the animal to roam outdoors. She could manage to hatch the eggs alone, but afterward she'd need help to catch enough insects to keep the little ones fed. She needed a father for them, and had less than two weeks to try to find one before the helpless nestlings came into the world.

She perched on a branch near her nesting cavity, occasionally darting out to snap up a passing insect. Then, things started to look up. She heard a male singing near the top of the adjacent sycamore tree. As luck would have it, he was unmated.

As she flitted from branch to branch, coming closer to him with each move, the striking black and white male became more animated. Her suitor was willing to invest some time in courting her, but she had no patience right now for the usual courtship protocol. Instead, she simply lowered herself into a posture that let him know she fancied him. He darted over and accepted her invitation to mount her. It was almost too easy.

Even though she was no longer fertile, she continued to copulate with him, and successfully completed the incubation of her eggs while he lingered nearby. She had pulled off the deception beautifully. The male assumed that the eggs were his, because, as far as he could tell, he was the only one that had been sexually involved with her since they met. As a result, he would work tirelessly to feed the babies when they hatched . . . never suspecting that he had been duped by an expectant mother into believing that he was the father of her unborn children.

Most females who are widowed or deserted aren't as lucky as this pied flycatcher. Bluffing of this sort works best during or immediately after the clutch of eggs is laid, although there have been cases in which males adopted the just-hatched broods of their newly-acquired mates.

Marriage entrapment hasn't been specifically studied in many bird species, but has been documented in the pied flycatcher and the savannah sparrow. Usually, the replacement male, whether he is seduced or is the seducer, doesn't stay around long enough to be useful. Occasionally, however, a female gets a commitment from him, as this one did.

It's analogous to a woman, early in her pregnancy and deserted by the baby's father, convincing another man that the child she's carrying is his. If he's slept with her, and thinks he's the only one who has, he won't have reason to suspect otherwise. He may even propose marriage.

Working together with the finesse of well-rehearsed dancers, male long-tailed manakins double-team a female, mutually seducing her for the benefit of just one of them.

KELLY AND ASTAIRE: THE BUDDY SYSTEM

The female visitor selected a comfortable place to sit and watch as the two fellows who had invited her to their bachelor pad went into their dance routine, directing it wholeheartedly at her. They were renowned for their athleticism and precision, and she found it all terribly thrilling as they vaulted over each other.

She wasn't born yesterday, though, and she sensed the motive behind the dazzling duo's performance was seduction, and that she'd probably end up having a one-night stand with one or the other. She had no illusions that this might lead to a long-term relationship with either of the confirmed bachelors.

The show they put on was exhilarating, and after a while, she found herself so caught up in it that she rose and began executing a few of her own moves, although her choreography wasn't as sophisticated as theirs. Seeing her get into the spirit of things spurred them to accelerate to a dizzying finale.

At last, the older of the two gave a signal to the other entertainer, who gracefully took his leave. Now alone with her, the remaining dancer changed to a slower, more seductive rhythm, moving in a circle around her. She was in ecstasy, and her body language told him, "Take me, I'm yours."

He did.

The lady involved is a long-tailed manakin, sitting at one end of a perch in a display court belonging to the two males. She had been drawn in by their call, sung in unison and perfectly synchronized, so that it reverberated through the dense Costa Rican forest.

The males, black with vivid blue backs, resplendent red crowns and fabulously long tail streamers, had formed a partnership the previous year for the express purpose of using their coordinated efforts to court females. They would continue this arrangement as long as both were alive.

They had worked out, early in their relationship, which was the dominant of the two, and therefore which would be the one to do the breeding. The subordinate male stood a good chance of inheriting their courting area eventually, and then joining up with another male over whom he would be dominant.

After the female's arrival, the males began their dance, which gave the impression of a revolving ferris wheel. Facing her, they took turns rising off the branch, hovering there, and then flying backward. After the first bird jumped up, the second one moved forward into the just-vacated spot to wait his turn. He jumped up as the first bird was landing behind him. Sometimes the sequence is repeated up to a hundred times, picking up speed as it continues, until it hits a frenetic pace.

At about that time, the female, having reached quite a state of excitement herself, starts flicking her wings and hopping up and down on her perch.

Eventually, the subordinate male flies off after a flutter and a vocal cue from his superior. The principal male then delivers a solo performance consisting of extremely slow-paced flights from one perch to the next, circling the aroused female and finally mounting her.

Afterward, she leaves to build her nest, incubate the eggs, and raise the youngsters entirely on her own.

The two males, meanwhile, will resume their synchronized calls, hoping to attract another female. One may arrive momentarily, or several days may pass before they enjoy the company of another female.

Cooperative courtship such as this, in which two, or sometimes three, males coordinate their efforts for the sake of one, is highly unusual in the bird world, but variations of it are the custom in certain manakin species.

It's a little like two buddies, both strikingly handsome and superb dancers, who spend the evening at a nightclub flirting with a girl who is obviously enjoying their company. They offer her a ride home, and while one is driving, the other is in the back seat making out with her.

THE WORLD'S OLDEST PROFESSION

Flying through the banana trees, the female hummingbird came across a profusion of delectable-looking banana flowers. Seeing them made her realize how hungry she was. It hadn't been easy finding good food sources during the winter. The best feeding territories were fiercely defended by highly territorial males that banished any of their species, male or female, that happened to trespass. That left poor pickings for many of the females.

Still, it was worth a try to get at the sweet nectar hidden in the flowers. She had been allowed to feed in the territory of another male, and the same ploy might work for her here.

Boldly, she flew to the most tempting flower, but before she could dip her long bill into its neck, the resident male seemed to come out of nowhere, chasing her off his territory. When she had been effectively expelled, he veered back to continue his border patrol.

She hovered for a moment and then, with all the determination of a wretched street urchin grappling for a discarded scrap of food, darted straight back. Four more times they repeated this routine, until the plucky little female raced back to the territory, arriving before the male.

Returning a few seconds later, the guard bird sat on his favorite perch and eyed her as she fed hungrily, but he didn't chase her this time. His attitude was moderating. He was no longer looking at her strictly as an invader; he was beginning to see her as a potential sex object.

After her hunger was satisfied, she flew over to his perch, and as she landed he lifted off and moved to another. She replaced him on that perch, too. It appeared that, for the time being, she had dominance over him in his own territory.

Finally, she briefly hovered back and forth in front of him and then settled next to him on the perch. That's when he went into action. He sprang up from his place on her right, passed over her head, and landed to her left. Then, he repeated it in the opposite direction – a really slick move for a guy who was at least a month away from the start of his breeding season.

Next, he did the hovering, back and forth in front of her, showing off the jewel-like purplish-red iridescence of his throat. She'd seen it all before, but indulged him by keeping her head turning to follow his movement. When he was ready, the female crouched on the branch as the male hovered behind and then lowered himself onto her back. She twisted her tail out of the way to make it easier for him, and an instant later carnal contact was made.

He was quickly finished with her, and flew off to a nearby perch. The female smoothed her feathers back into place, and then started to make another pass at the banana flowers. The male, however, had paid her in advance for her services by allowing her to get her fill of nectar, and she wasn't going to wheedle more from him now. He once again assumed dominance and firmly saw her off.

Prostitution behavior among hummingbirds during the nonbreeding season was first reported by Dr. Larry Wolf, Syracuse University, based on his observations of purple-throated carib hummingbirds in the British West Indies. Examinations of the birds showed that neither was yet in breeding condition: the females were not ready to lay eggs, and the males were not capable of fertilizing them. It might seem, then, that neither would have any interest in sexual activity. Yet, there was a pay-for-sex system being exploited by some males and females that he studied.

Another case of food for sex involves ospreys. While female ospreys are incubating, they are fed by their mates, who bring fish to the nest. If the male is negligent and the female is hungry, she might start to beg food from other males as they fly over. One female that was always hungry was known to mosey over to another nest, not far away, where a single male was in residence. There, the male gave her food in exchange for sex.

Pity the poor male corncrake, a close relative of the sora rail and coot, who tried 23 times to copulate with a researcher's stuffed specimen of a female corncrake, but was getting nowhere. Before trying again, he left for a short while, and when he returned, he was carrying a luscious, juicy caterpillar which he tried to give to her. Still no response. Even paying for sex didn't work for this handsome little guy.

MARRIED LIFE

Geese and swans are renowned for loyalty to their mates, but none surpasses the Bewick's swan for lifelong marital fidelity. Divorce is extremely rare for these devoted pairs, even when they fail to raise any young during their long lives.

TILL DEATH DO US PART

To the minds of most people, the ideal romantic relationship is a traditional one. A man and woman meet, court, and the longer they know each other, the more certain they are that they have found their soulmate.

After a fairly lengthy engagement, they tie the knot. He finds a spot that he thinks is ideal for their new home, and successfully fends off other interested parties who have set their sites on it, too. Then, working together, the newlyweds begin building.

They remain side by side, through the good times and the bad, putting up a united front against any threat. Divorce or extra-marital relationships are never contemplated by either partner.

Over the years of their long life together, the couple may successfully raise a number of children. Or, they may be unlucky in this respect, and end their lives without a single offspring. Nevertheless, they remain together for the rest of their days.

So it is in the life of the Bewick's swan.

For nearly all swan species, as well as most geese and many ducks, auks, puffins, cranes, storks, and some others, long-term monogamy is the preferred relationship. However, few demonstrate the fidelity of the Bewick's swan.

At the Wildfowl and Wetlands Trust in Slimbridge, near the estuary of England's Severn River, swans have been studied intently for nearly 50 years. In all that time, the researchers have found not a single case of divorce among Bewick's swan pairs that had successfully raised young. Failure to reproduce is a leading cause of divorce in birds, but even among a thousand pairs of Bewick's that never managed to breed successfully, there were only 20 divorces.

Wild swans probably survive an average of 12 years, although one was known to have lived at least 26 years. The longer a swan lives, the greater the likelihood that it will outlive its mate. When one member of the pair dies, the widow or widower might eventually take a new mate. However, they don't rush into a new relationship, and often take two or more years to find an acceptable partner. Some don't remate for as long as six years after the death of a spouse.

For swans, fidelity translates into more offspring being produced during their lifetime. At Slimbridge, it was found that the longer a pair stays together, the more young they raise each year, with their success rate gradually increasing over their first eight years together.

In addition, pairs are more successful than individuals at winning prime feeding spots. If challenged, a pair almost invariably will oust an individual. When the dispute over a food source or a nesting site is between two pairs, it's usually up to the males to fight it out, with the females and any cygnets taking on the roles of cheerleaders.

Traditional sex roles are reversed in red phalaropes, with the uninhibited female aggressively pursuing the smaller male. If other females attempt to abduct her mate, she'll do her best to shield him with her body while trying to fend them off.

MR. MOM AND THE
EMANCIPATED WOMAN

I t was a long journey from the warm ocean east of South America to this spot on the arctic tundra. Now, in early June, the male red phalarope has finally spotted what he traveled all this way to find. It's a patch of tundra dotted with small pools among mossy hummocks and tufts of grass into which his dull plumage will blend imperceptibly — the perfect place to find a mate and raise a family. There are a few other birds in the area, but it is still early, and this prime piece of real estate remains relatively unoccupied.

He lands on one of the ponds and begins to feed on tiny crustaceans and insects. Then, as if his prayers had been answered, he hears a female calling to him from above, advertising her availability. He looks up to see her flying in circles, the low angle of the arctic sun accentuating the rich coloring of her reddish underparts. Still calling, she lands on the pond, swims around him, and then rises up on another circling flight. The ritual continues until he starts to swim after her, following where she leads.

Abruptly, the couple's tranquillity is shattered by the onslaught of three other females flying relentlessly toward them, shrieking. Each one is looking for a mate, and each is hell-bent on having this newly-arrived bachelor for her own.

More timid than his larger fiancé, the male rushes to her, closes his eyes and hunkers down while she spreads her wings to cover him and protect him from their assailants. She fights just as fiercely as the intruders, but one of them is particularly aggressive, and eventually drives her back. The conqueror then takes up the position of the vanquished, covering the male with her own wings. The defeated female, along with the two remaining members of the raiding party, eventually have to concede the fight. Exhausted, they take their leave, bits of feather and down still floating in the air.

To the victor go the spoils. In this case, it's the cowering male. On his very first day here, he found a choice plot for feeding, was courted by a handsome female, and, before they could consummate their relationship, was ruthlessly abducted by another. If he wanted to breed this year, it would have to be with this spitfire.

With things quiet again, he starts preening his disheveled feathers, trying to regain his composure. At last he's able to get a good look at Madame. He has to admire her pluckiness, and now that her fury has subsided, he can see that she is every bit as handsome as his former companion. His optimism returns.

The triumphant female swims around him, twittering softly, beckoning him. He succumbs, signaling their engagement.

During the following days, she can't seem to take her eyes off him. As a matter of fact, if she loses sight of him, she calls urgently until he is again twittering at her side. His soft apologies are sometimes cut short with a sharp yelp in response to a less-than-loving stab from the bill of his betrothed. She has become something of an avian Miss Piggy, admonishing him to stay in line with her own version of, "Watch it, Buster." He resigns himself to this with a "Yes, dear" demeanor.

Seemingly inseparable now, they make a joint decision on where the nest will be located. Together, they scrape out a depression which the male lines with grasses.

With a home for their eggs now built, the pair is finally ready to consummate their marriage. There are some quiet twitters, then the female rises up and whirs her wings before settling down in a slightly crouched position. The male climbs onto her back, sometimes having to flap his wings to keep his balance, and their cloacas meet. It is only a quickie. In less than ten seconds, it is all over, and they both turn their attention to feeding again. One might think they are blushing, a little embarrassed by what they have just done. Not likely; they're at it again in another five minutes.

The next morning, the male stands by and watches as the female lays her first egg in the nest. On each of the next three days, she lays another egg, never spending more than about 15 minutes at a time at the nest.

Seeing the eggs causes him to become increasingly interested in the nest—and less attentive to her. After the last egg is laid, he devotes himself full-time to the nest and eggs. His wife, on the other hand, is still in the mood for courting, but not in the mood for tending to a home and family. She slips away, ready to start advertising again: UPF (unattached phalarope female) seeking docile SPM (single phalarope male) who respects emancipated women. Her absence doesn't seem to distress her deserted spouse, who is contentedly incubating their eggs.

When the young hatch, they will be bright-eyed and ready to leave the nest almost immediately. Their father won't need to feed them, because they can do that for themselves. He will, however, cover them, when necessary, with the warmth of his body during the few days before they are entirely self-sufficient.

Meanwhile, Mama's got another sweetie. Her new mate responded to her advertising flight only hours after his nest had been destroyed by gulls. The extreme shortness of the nesting season in the tundra doesn't allow the luxury of any leisure time between nestings.

Because this female got an early start this year and is aggressive in getting what she wants, she may have time to quickly recycle once more after deserting her second husband. If so, she might lay a third set of eggs with yet another husband before tiring of it all and returning to the ocean and heading south again in the first week of July.

The males remain for an additional month, hatching the young. Last to leave are the youngsters themselves. Now abandoned by both parents and entirely on their own, they set off with some miraculous innate sense of knowing not only that they must leave, but also where they must go.

Red-necked phalaropes have turned the tables on traditional male and female roles. It even confused Audubon, who identified phalarope males as the more colorful, larger females and vice versa in his paintings.

Phalarope males assume all the domestic chores, except for actually laying the eggs. The females are the aggressors, have brighter breeding plumage, and take little interest in the nest and eggs. In addition, female phalaropes can be sequentially polyandrous, taking different mates in succession, while their deserted husbands raise the kids.

Both male and female hormones are produced in all birds. But in phalaropes and other role-reversed species, the females get a higher than normal dose of male hormones, which promote aggressiveness and bring about the more colorful breeding plumage. The males get a higher than normal dose of female hormones, which stimulate incubation behavior and the development of brood patches. A brood patch is an area on the abdomen from which the feathers drop and the skin swells with an enriched supply of blood before incubation begins. The bird, normally a female, puts the brood patch directly against the eggs to warm them with her body heat. In phalaropes, the male develops the brood patches, one on each side.

Being master of a harem may seem like a dream come true to some men, but the male red-winged blackbird knows that it's not easy maintaining several squabbling, competitive wives.

LIFE IN A HAREM

From his vantage point at the top of an old cattail on a fine spring morning, the male red-winged blackbird surveyed his realm: a particularly prime piece of marsh at the end of a small lake and a harem of four wives, all busy putting finishing touches on their well-concealed nests or in the process of laying eggs.

He really would like to have added a few more to his harem. His territory could certainly handle the additional nests and provide enough food for the extra mouths that would have to be fed. And he has a sex drive strong enough to meet the demand.

His wives, however, saw things differently, and prohibited any others of their sex from settling in their domain, and with their man. Any that tried were quickly chased away.

Each wife had her own space to construct her nest. She kept strangers out, and also ensured that her harem sisters didn't intrude. Terribly competitive with one another, squabbles broke out frequently. But, when they were all behaving themselves and didn't have their knickers in a twist over something or other, life was quite pleasant for their lord and master.

He spent his days at the top of a gently swaying cattail or small willow. In his constant effort to sustain control of his territory, he repeatedly sang a gurgling *kong-a-ree* and displayed his badge of authority, dazzling red epaulets edged with sunny yellow. From time to time, he'd risk making a quick foray to a bird feeder at one of the lake houses, but he was never away for more than a few minutes.

Maintaining a choice territory and a harem was unquestionably desirable, but it wasn't all a bed of roses. He could never relax his vigilance. If he was away too long, a neighboring male could take advantage of the opportunity and sneak in to sample the delights of his harem. He knew this was a possibility, because he had done it himself when other males had left their females unattended.

In a few days, when all eggs had been laid and all his wives were incubating, things would quiet down a little. The females would be past their fertile stage, and even if another male got to them, the rogue would no longer be able to father any illegitimate offspring.

Things would get hectic again when the chicks hatched. It was unlikely that none of the nests would be destroyed before then, but if by some stroke of luck all went well, there could be 16 tiny nestlings demanding to be fed and kept clean. He could help the mothers, like some of his buddies did, but considered that sort of thing to be woman's work. Besides, no matter how much he did, they'd want more.

Maybe four wives was enough after all.

Red-winged and yellow-headed blackbirds are among the few bird species in which a male acquires a harem of females and remains with them through the breeding season.

The extent of parental assistance varies greatly among individual redwing males, and perhaps regionally, too. Some may not participate at all in feeding young and removing fecal sacs (the avian equivalent of disposable diapers). Others take their paternal responsibilities quite seriously.

Female redwings are attracted to the habitat, although it is logical that the best males would claim and be able to maintain ownership of the best territories.

Size and quality of a territory influences the size of a harem, to some extent. A redwing male may have only one wife, or in exceptional cases, as many as 15, but three or four is more typical. Another limiting factor to harem size is the females themselves. They don't make it easy for another female to become a member of their sorority.

Some birds, notably wild turkeys and ring-necked pheasants, may also attract groups of females, but only for short-term relationships. After breeding, those females go off to build a nest and raise their family without any help from the males.

Having two husbands works to the advantage of the female Galapagos hawk, enabling her to lay more eggs and raise more young during her lifetime than if she had only one husband.

MÉNAGE À TROIS

For a lot of men, the ultimate sexual fantasy is a ménage à trois, with two women making love to him at the same time. For a lot of women, it's having two men make love to her.

Those women might envy the female Galapagos hawk, who may spend her entire adult life with two lovers – although she doesn't go in for anything kinky. She'll only take on one male at a time.

All members of Galapagos hawk threesomes appear to willingly share family responsibilities, and live together amicably year after year. The female definitely derives the greatest benefit from the arrangement. Both males are her lovers, and assist her unhesitatingly in raising the offspring that result from their unions, regardless of who fathered them.

All three take turns incubating the two eggs that she normally produces, and when the chicks hatch, both males hunt for provisions to bring back to the nest. The mother usually stays with the young chicks while the fathers go hunting for a choice marine iguana or other suitable prey to bring home.

While their arrangement may seem somewhat unorthodox, no one can argue with the fact that it works for them. Compared to Galapagos hawks that nest in pairs, the trios produce more eggs and raise more young.

About half of all Galapagos hawk nests are occupied by a female with more than one mate. They are one of only three species in which one female typically nests with more than one male. Generally in these situations, the habitat or the number of females available means that the males have a choice of either being part of a trio, or not breeding at all.

Another of the ménage à trois species is the Harris' hawk, in which 50 percent of the nests in southern Arizona were occupied by a male and two females. Here, too, nesting success was greater for the threesomes than it was for pairs.

The third species is a flightless rail, the Tasmanian native hen, which establishes life-long breeding groups, sometimes of pairs, but often of three birds that characteristically include two brothers and an unrelated female.

Two-males-to-one-female combinations also occur frequently in the dunnock, or hedge sparrow. In this species, the two males are fierce rivals for copulations with their mate, rather than congenial cohorts like those above.

A trio in opposite proportions is often found in the magpie goose, when a male may have two females as his permanent mates. The two females deposit their eggs into a single nest, and all three parents share incubation duties and the rearing of the goslings.

Jacanas turn the tables on sex roles. Some females acquire harems of three or more males, each of which assumes the traditionally female tasks of nest building, incubation and chick rearing. Meanwhile, his polyandrous wife keeps a protective vigil on her territory and multiple husbands.

THE FEMALE FANTASY:
A MALE HAREM

J ust north of the Mexican border, on a marshy lake in the Rio Grande delta, a male northern jacana daintily steps from one lily pad to another, deftly snapping up insects from the floating vegetation as he moves along. The exceptional length of both his toes and his toenails distributes his weight evenly over the water lilies, allowing him to progress without having to worry about sinking into the water.

Appetite satisfied, he scurries back to his nest. He's been away from the eggs long enough.

His fatherly role began in April, when the small yet desirable territory that he had claimed for himself and managed to defend from other males had been penetrated by an enterprising female. At first glance, she didn't look much different from him. They both were adorned in the same dark colors, but he couldn't help noticing that she was quite large. That's okay; he likes big women. In fact, he likes them very big. This one outweighed him by about 75 percent.

It wasn't long before he realized that her intentions were twofold. She wanted his territory, but she meant to have him, too. She pursued him aggressively, making it clear that she was ready to enter into a sexual relationship with him. He was a little intimidated by her, yet drawn to her, too. Perhaps instinctively he knew it was unlikely that this amazon would allow any other female to get near him, so he accepted her overtures.

Their courtship was simple, but graceful, as each bird raised its shiny maroon wings over its back to flash the bright greenish yellow patches. When she lowered herself, enabling him to mount her, he must have been grateful that she didn't want to be on top.

For her part, the female didn't mind that her new mate was smaller than she. He was relatively quiet and cooperative, and not afraid to show his feminine side. She liked that in a guy, needed it, really.

Over the next few days, they made love frequently, usually at her instigation, and she oversaw his construction of a simple nest. He was not a talented architect, and what he came up with was really no more than a floating raft of vegetation, with just enough structure to keep the eggs from rolling into the water. Into this, on successive days, she laid four beautiful eggs, glossy brown with fine black scrolling. Then, she lost interest in the nest and wandered off, but not far.

Meanwhile, the male settled down to the task of incubating the eggs on his own and eventually looking after the chicks when they hatched.

On the third day after she left, the male spotted a purple gallinule getting dangerously close to the nest and eggs while he was taking a short lunch break. Alarmed, he put himself between the nest and the tres-passer. Crouching, he opened his wings to emphasize the sharp yellow spur at the bend of each, and started screaming. A moment later, his mate was there, swooping at the intruder and striking it with her feet as she passed. Together, the pair ousted the gallinule, a major predator of jacana eggs and chicks.

A few days later, the interloper was a male jacana overstepping the boundary from an adjacent territory. Once again, the female responded to her mate's screams and helped him convince the neighbor that he should return to his own turf. Minutes later, she also departed, this time flying directly to the territory of the male that she had just helped evict. He was, after all, another of her husbands, and she was in the process of laying another clutch of four eggs for him to tend.

In the meantime, she was also making visits, almost on a daily basis, to the other two males that completed her harem. She had acquired all of them as mates when she laid claim to a large territory that encom-passed the four males' smaller territories. Adept at juggling her consorts, she was sometimes able to make love to all of them in a single day. However, as soon as a male began incubating, she dropped him as a sex partner. When the chicks got to be several weeks old and she could hold his attention once more, she'd probably start courting him again and get him to start another nest.

Jacanas are among the only one or two percent of bird species worldwide that practice polyandry, in which a female has more than one mate. About half of them are shorebirds.

Jacanas are simultaneously polyandrous: a female might have several males in her territory, with all of them on different clutches of her eggs at the same time. The number of males in her harem depends on the size of the territory she defends. If a male's territory is large, she may have only him as a mate and be monogamous, but three males to one female is more common, and there may be as many as five males.

White-winged trumpeters, large South American birds that fall in size between cranes and rails, also engage in simultaneous polyandry with a different twist. They form breeding groups in which only the dominant female lays eggs, but all the males in the group, perhaps three, compete to copulate with her, often interrupting each other's attempts. Up to 90 percent of all copulation attempts are disrupted by rival group members during the female's fertile period. She seems to be receptive to the attentions of any of the males, no matter which rung they occupy on the group's social ladder.

All the males help raise the brood that hatches from her single clutch of eggs. Other females in these groups seem to be those that have not reached sexual maturity. They might engage in sex with some of the subordinate males if they manage to do it out of sight of the dominant male and female, but they apparently do not lay eggs.

Polyandry is quite rare in birds, and until 1972, there were only two documented cases in wild birds, one in the flightless gallinule and one in a jacana. Since then, many more examples have been, and are continuing to be, verified.

Mixed marriages may not draw much attention anymore in people, but among birds, they are quite rare, and liaisons such as this union of a red crossbill and pine siskin never fail to pique the interest of the scientific community.

BIRDS OF A DIFFERENT FEATHER: MIXED MARRIAGES

You catch sight of them as they walk toward you in the mall, and you try not to be obvious about having noticed them. Still, you can't help yourself, even though relationships like theirs ceased to be a novelty to you long ago. It's just that they are such a striking couple, she a petite blonde with a peaches-and-cream complexion, he a handsome contrast with his curly black hair and ebony skin.

These days, mixed race couples barely draw a glance anymore, let alone a raised eyebrow. On the other hand, it is so rare in birds that when it happens it still sparks a flurry of scientific interest and journal reports.

Usually, ornithologists find out about cross-breeding in birds only because they happen upon a hybrid offspring. Often, a hybrid is the product of a union between two very closely related species, such as the mallard and black duck. Every now and then, however, the experts come across one that may stump them for a little while. That's what happened in the early 1980s, when a pine siskin and a red crossbill met, mated, and produced at least one youngster. Though we can only guess, let's say the crossbill was the male and the siskin the female.

It might have been a case of mistaken identity, or even rape. If the male red crossbill didn't look too closely, or if his eyesight wasn't too keen, he might have mistaken the female siskin for a petite female of his own species, but that's a stretch. The two females are hardly look-alikes. And she could scarcely mistake the red male with the strange overbite for a male of her species, any more than a female American robin might mistake a male northern cardinal for a potential mate.

Perhaps it was just an impetuous one-time dalliance, and the two were already paired with others of their species, or soon would be. If so, the pine siskin's husband must have suspected something when the large chick that eventually hatched in their nest didn't bear a strong resemblance to him.

Or, perhaps the siskin and crossbill felt a strong mutual attraction and ignored the fact that they were from two different genera, possibly staying together as man and wife through the rearing of their offspring.

Well, c'est l'amour. No one really knows how it happened, or why, only that it did, because the proof was in the progeny. Their daughter was seen feeding among a flock of pine siskins, but not really with them, in the South Dakota backyard of Dr. Dan Tallman of Northern State College, Aberdeen. Her lineage was determined shortly afterward by Dr. Richard Zusi at the National Museum of Natural History, Smithsonian Institution.

Where their breeding ranges overlap, red-shafted and yellow-shafted flickers interbreed frequently. In fact, the two are now regarded as one species. Frequent interbreeding between the Baltimore and the Bullock's oriole made ornithologists take another look at them, too. Both names were changed to northern oriole for several years, but are again separate species.

Some of the most famous hybrids may be the Brewster's and Lawrence's warblers, which are the result of matings between blue-winged and golden-winged warblers.

There may be more trysts between species than anyone can prove, because unless they result in hybrid offspring that can be collected and identified, there is rarely any evidence.

In most cases, even copulations between birds of the same species aren't easily observed, so there are precious few eyewitness accounts of birds of a different feather getting it on. One involved a pair of rusty-margined flycatchers and a pair of ruddy ground doves that were perched nearby. When the male dove flew away, the male flycatcher impertinently flew over to the female dove and successfully copulated with her, apparently in full view of his own mate. This really whetted scientific interest, because not only do these two species belong to different families (Tyrant Flycatcher Family and Pigeon Family), but also to different orders (Passeriformes and Columbiformes). In other words, they aren't even remotely related, except that they're both birds.

Another outrageous twosome involved a house sparrow male that repeatedly made love to a brown-headed cowbird, also a male.

Their motives may be different than ours, but dunnocks often indulge in foreplay. In fact, these somewhat dull-plumaged hedge sparrows have quite a colorful sex life.

FOREPLAY

Having just chased away his rival, the male dunnock now has his mate all to himself and he's in the mood for love. The object of his desire is almost always in the mood, but he believes a little foreplay can reap great rewards.

She's already crouching in front of him with fluffed feathers and quivering wings, lifting her tail to reveal her goodies. Excited, the male hops from side to side behind her, then approaches and starts to peck under her tail. After almost two minutes and nearly 100 pecks, the female's cloaca becomes quite pink and distended. This looks like pretty rough sex play, verging on sado-masochism, yet the female doesn't seem to mind.

Finally, he achieves the desired effect. Her cloaca starts pumping strongly, and she ejects a small amount of fluid. As soon as she does, he's on her, their cloacas merge, and in less than a second, he's all finished.

If they were people, they might be asking each other, "Was it good for you?"

Dunnocks are just drab little hedge sparrows – until you start to look at their love life. Any color they lack in plumage is more than made up for in their extremely colorful sex lives.

Dunnocks indulge in many of the behaviors described in this book: ménage à trois, adultery, bigamy, polygynandry, and mate guarding, to name a few.

The male dunnock customarily pecks his mate's cloaca prior to copulation, and the most plausible explanation is that it forces her to expel any stored sperm that might not be his.

When two males are mated to one female – a fairly common occurrence in dunnocks – the competition between the two males is intense. Each wants to assure he is the father of the female's brood, and does all he can to prevent the other from copulating with her through mate guarding and chasing away his rival. The last male to breed with her has the highest chance of fertilizing the next egg she lays. If he gets her to eject sperm, possibly that of another male, before he inseminates her, it may further increase the likelihood of his paternity.

The female, on the other hand, approaches both males for copulation, because if each believes that at least some of the chicks are his, he is more likely to help her feed them. In cases where only the primary male bred with the female, the secondary male never fed the nestlings.

Gannets seem to enjoy scratching each other's necks and heads, just as we appreciate having our backs scratched or our shoulders rubbed by our mates.

DARLING, WILL YOU SCRATCH MY BACK?

A little lower. Still lower. Now a little to the left. That's it . . . aah. The northern gannet is getting her head and the back of her neck scratched and cleaned by her mate. She stretches her neck out in front of him and ruffles the feathers, inviting him to start on another spot, back where she can't reach with her own bill. Eyes closed, she obviously finds it utterly blissful.

A soothing massage, a stimulating back rub, or just having someone scratch that itchy spot you can't reach can be heavenly. Some birds enjoy it, too, particularly parrots, cormorants, herons and egrets, pigeons and doves, penguins, and a few songbirds.

When a bird grooms the inaccessible areas of another's neck and head, it's called allopreening. Between mates, it reinforces the pair bond, and, in some cases, can alleviate aggression within a pair.

No matter how faithful his wife may be, this male magpie will not let her out of his sight. A rival may try to seduce her if he relaxes his vigil, so he closely guards her throughout the day.

SLIP INTO THIS CHASTITY BELT, DEAR: POSSESSIVENESS

They are inseparable. Everywhere she goes, he follows. He gives the impression that he can't live without her, and that his actions are simply an expression of ardent devotion.

His behavior, however, is not driven by affection, but by blatant self-interest. Wildly jealous, unreasonably suspicious, and convinced that his ostensibly faithful spouse will cheat on him at the first opportunity, the excessively vigilant husband shadows her constantly.

For the most part, the male magpie's fears are without foundation. His mate has shown no inclination to seek the attentions of other males. On the contrary, she has been a model of fidelity. However, he realizes that if he lets his guard down, a nearby male might sneak in and try to seduce her.

She will start laying eggs in another day or two, and he wants every assurance that all of the chicks he will help her raise are his, not someone else's little bastards. So, he spends nearly every waking moment with his mate to prevent the possibility of being cuckolded.

For the time being, the male magpie's motto is, "Whither thou goest, I will go."

Mate guarding, as this is called, is found in many bird species, including ducks, swallows, finches and others. It's practiced by some human couples, too, whether justified or merely a consequence of irrational insecurities.

In birds, mate guarding is often warranted. A male magpie that had been on guard duty was overcome with drowsiness and allowed himself to nod off. Seconds later, a neighboring male darted in and tried to draw the female into adultery. The dozing male quickly roused to attack the intruder, chasing him off.

In northern cardinals, mate guarding can be very effective, almost the avian equivalent of locking on a chastity belt. The number of offspring belonging to males other than the resident male is less in cardinals than in many other songbirds. Cardinal males average more than 70 percent of their time staying close to their mates when the females are fertile, but some are with them 100 percent of the time. The more time they devote to mate guarding, the lower the risk of cuckoldry. In one study, the only case of illegitimate young in a cardinal nest occurred where a male escorted his mate less than 20 percent of the time.

Some species, in which it is impossible for the male to continuously guard his mate, use frequent copulations to try to assure their paternity.

Raptors, for example, may have to range far to hunt. In these cases, it's not unusual for copulation to take place within a minute of the pair's reunion.

Sperm competition is the reason for all this obsessive possessiveness. It is generally believed that the last sperm a female receives has the greatest chance of fertilizing her eggs. Therefore, if a female does cheat on her mate, he may be able to protect his paternity by copulating with her afterwards. For this reason, when a hen duck is raped, her mate will immediately attempt to copulate with her himself.

The most critical time for mate guarding is usually during the week or so before the first egg is laid, continuing until the clutch is complete.

WHEN THE HONEYMOON IS OVER

Adultery is now known to be far more rampant among birds than anyone had ever imagined. Many birds may be monogamous, but that doesn't mean they won't have an extra-marital fling, like this Baltimore oriole.

ADULTERY I:
"SHE MEANT NOTHING TO ME, HONEST!"

Well hidden along a branch of a maple tree, a female Baltimore oriole sits in her pouchlike nest, patiently incubating four pale bluish white eggs blotched with brown. To the right and a little below, her mate has been singing his distinctive song most of the day, although he has stopped now, and seems to have wandered off. It is late in the afternoon, and time for her to feed. She doesn't like to leave the nest unguarded, but stealthily slips away nevertheless.

She'll stop off for some fast food first, at one of the orange halves on offer behind one of the houses down the road. As she approaches, she hears a few notes of song, not much, yet enough to recognize that it's her mate. Then she spots him . . . but at the moment he's not interested in the orange. He's trysting with the female that lives next door!

Similar scenarios are played out around the world every day during the breeding season, many more times than anyone had imagined.

Actually, the majority of bird species are monogamous . . . more or less. Some are monogamous only for the time it takes to raise one brood, others for a breeding season, some for a lifetime. Even so, most of these birds, especially the males, will try to get a little on the side.

Very often, such fleeting liaisons go unnoticed, even by experienced observers. Yet, DNA fingerprinting has proven that there is a shocking amount of hanky panky going on.

Until recently, it was assumed that any chicks in the nest of a monogamous pair were the offspring of those two parents. Then, new scientific techniques became available that could show researchers whether or not a male had been dallying with his neighbor's wife. Very recently, DNA fingerprinting has been added to the ornithologists' arsenal, giving them a reliable method of finding out if those illicit liaisons actually result in any illegitimate children.

Indeed they do. In an investigation of tree swallows, DNA evidence revealed that 38 percent of the nestlings were the result of what biologists call extra-pair copulations (adultery). In fact, in one nest, none of the six offspring had been fathered by the resident male.

Scandalous, too, are the antics of the monogamous superb fairy-wrens of Australia. DNA tests found that 95 percent of the nests in one study contained at least one baby that was not the fathered by the mother's mate. In all, more than three-quarters of the chicks tested did not belong to the male that was raising them.

Extra-marital flings also seem to be common in polygamous birds, like red-winged blackbirds, where one male may be mated to several females. It is not unusual to find that about half of the nests of red-winged blackbirds contain one or more chicks whose real father is the male in a neighboring territory. Infidelity is so rampant among redwings, in fact, that more than 20 percent of the young produced by the average male are the result of matings with females other than those in his own harem.

In one of the more interesting field studies, some of the males in a red-winged blackbird colony underwent vasectomies. They could still copulate and defend their territories, but were incapable of fertilizing eggs. Yet, for quite a while after the males had been sterilized (as long as 40 days), their mates continued to lay fertile eggs.

As studies continue, the list of birds that engage in adultery keeps growing. It has now been reported in every family of birds, although certainly not in every species. A few of the ones known to cheat on their spouses range from backyard favorites like Baltimore orioles, indigo buntings and eastern bluebirds, to acorn woodpeckers, white-crowned sparrows and bobolinks, to more exotic types like rock ptarmigans and white ibises.

For some, it's rare, and may simply be the result of an opportunity presenting itself. For others, it's an important part of their breeding tactics. If a male can fertilize eggs in addition to those of his mate, he has a better chance of passing his genes on to more offspring. He is, as we say, pursuing a mixed reproductive strategy.

ADULTERY II: "I'M NO PUSHOVER, BUT . . ."

From her vantage point above the birdhouse in the apple tree, the female black-capped chickadee watches her mate begin to deftly open a sunflower seed on the tube feeder less than 20 feet away.

Throughout their courtship and while she worked on the nest in the birdhouse, he has been very attentive to her. In fact, he rarely lets her out of his sight. Still, he isn't the most desirable male in the neighborhood. That would be the male whose fine territory adjoins theirs, in the adjacent backyard.

Now was her chance. With her mate's attention on the seed that he holds with his feet, she might be able to escape for a few minutes. That's all she'd need.

Flying quickly in the opposite direction from the bird feeders, she follows the sound of the neighboring male's voice, and spots him in the fencerow. There's no time for conventional courtship etiquette; she merely settles nearby and crouches, wings quivering, in the submissive posture that says she wants him.

He knows the message well. He is regarded as a high quality male, and several females other than his mate have sought him out for liaisons. He usually obliges, as he does with this female.

Then, as quickly as she arrived, she departs, and flies directly to the sunflower seed feeder where she last saw her mate. He joins her almost immediately, unaware that he has been cuckolded and that there is a good chance that the egg she will lay tomorrow has been fertilized by the neighborhood beau ideal.

Most female birds don't actively seek sexual encounters with males other than their mates. In a few species, however, including the black-capped chickadee, house sparrow, and tree swallows, there are some promiscuous females.

A male may practice mate guarding or try other tactics to avoid being cuckolded, since it's in his best interest to ensure that the young in whom he's investing so much time and effort are carrying his genes.

Interestingly, the term cuckold seems to have been in use at least since the 1400s, and perhaps even earlier, as a scornful label for the husband of an adulterous woman. It was supposedly derived from the cuckoo's habit of laying its eggs in another bird's nest.

For the female, there may be a number of reasons why she will either submit to or, in some cases, seek out extra-pair copulations. Getting a free dinner is one, because some males feed females before having sex.

Or, if she's committed to her current mate for only a single brood, she might be sizing up this male as a future mate. Another explanation is that perhaps she is taking precautions against the possibility that her mate may not be fertile or, like the chickadee above, is trying to raise the genetic quality of her offspring by mating with a male that is of higher quality than her own spouse.

Whatever her motives for accepting the advances of another male, or encouraging them, she must be discreet. If her mate believes that he is not the father of her children, he is less likely to devote as much energy to their defense and feeding as he would if they were his.

Frustrated male birds might resort to masturbation to satisfy their sexual urges. A hermit hummingbird, for example, may find a leaf growing at an angle that feels just right.

WILL I GO BLIND?

L ittle boys and girls used to be warned that they would go blind, or maybe get warts, if they masturbated. They were always greatly relieved when they discovered for themselves that this was not at all true. Birds, on the other hand, have never been inhibited by these cultural taboos.

Such was the case of the male sage grouse that had been strutting and dancing, his spiky tail flared and the air sacs on his breast making plopping sounds, every morning for more than a month. Alas, he was one of almost 30 males that were using the ancestral strutting ground in eastern Wyoming, and so far he had not had a single female interested in mating with him. Females visited the strutting ground every morning, shopping with discerning eyes for a suitable mate. But all the girls pretty much had the same taste in men, and this male was not among the two or three that were getting most of the action.

Still, seeing the hens did get him excited. To release his frustration, he strutted over to a nearby pile of earth. It was not exactly the size and shape of a hen, but it had been adequate for his purposes in the past and

would be again. He lowered himself onto it, and with a few quick move-
ments, he had relief.

And he didn't go blind.

Scientists often come up with quite prim terms for certain behaviors.
In this case, they refer to it as false mating, and sage grouse aren't the
only birds to indulge in it, although it does seem to be strictly a guy thing.

It's frequently reported in captive birds, and has also been observed
in a number of wild species, including American robins.

Probably most of the hermit hummingbird species masturbate,
because many have been caught in the act. The image one conjures up
of a wee hummingbird first performing his courtship for, and then forni-
cating with, a leaf is amusing but poignant, because these are most likely
young males who have no chance of mating with a female that year.
Often, the leaf or some other piece of vegetation hangs or is growing
upward at an angle that feels right to the hovering hummingbird and
sways easily underneath him. Once a good leaf is located, it will be used
time and again.

Researchers sometimes use stuffed specimens to check for sex recognition or species recognition in birds. Often, males, like this house wren, regard the inanimate dummy birds as potential sex partners, courting and then mounting them.

INFLATABLE DOLLS

Firmly ensconced in a suitable summer residence after his long migration, the male house wren is suddenly aware of another wren on a branch of the cherry tree near the center of his territory.

He initially takes it to be a male, because he has been on his territory for more than a week, and until now, no female wrens have arrived from the wintering grounds, only other males. This bird, however, does not challenge him in any way, as another male would certainly do, and, in fact, seems quite docile. It has to be a female.

Having endured most of the year in celibacy, the excited male is nearly beside himself with ecstasy. He assumes she must be desirous of a mate, because she does not retreat when he approaches in short flights, from the grape vine to the spruce, then from branch to branch in the cherry tree.

Still she holds her ground. She must find him very appealing. At last he is within inches of her, and still she does not flee. He flutters his wings tentatively, and is pleased to see that she is not showing any sign of rejecting him. On the other hand, she's not giving him much encouragement, either. He'd suffered some cool receptions from females before, but none had shown the stiff reserve of this one.

No matter. She might be a real dummy, but she's the best thing around at the moment. So, he hops onto her back and gets quick gratification, even though she's not at all responsive. It wasn't all that bad, though, and she didn't fly way, so after a few minutes, he's back for a repeat performance.

He must have been terribly disappointed when the researcher returned to the cherry tree to retrieve the stuffed specimen that had become the wren's sex toy.

Happily, a real female found him the following day.

Like this wren, men who resort to adult toys like inflatable dolls find them unresponsive, but perhaps better than nothing. If a real woman should come along and show interest, though, the valve is opened, and the doll deflated and relegated to the back of the closet.

When researchers have positioned female stuffed specimens near male birds, the males usually mount them, sometimes after performing their traditional courtship display.

If a real female appears on the scene, a male quickly loses interest in the dummy bird in favor of the animated one. The live female, meanwhile, is likely to try to beat the stuffing out of the model, literally, with ferocious pecks at the head and neck of her rival.

Stuffed birds have been used to test sex recognition in a number of species. Very inexperienced red-winged blackbirds that were beginning their first breeding season showed some confusion, and mounted not only male and female dummies of their own species, but also nearly every other species that was presented, including a male northern cardinal, a blue jay, a wood thrush, love birds, and meadowlarks, among others.

Experienced redwing males copulated only with female specimens of their own species, though showed some impatience when their passion was unrequited. One tried gently pecking at the base of the phony female's tail to motivate her.

Rape is brutal, and in birds it is often committed by groups of males. In mallards, a generally monogamous species, rape is so widespread that nearly half of all broods are fathered by more than one male.

THE GANG BANG

In some species of birds, an otherwise devoted husband may turn into a frightening assailant of other's wives. Sometimes, he'll become part of a band of thugs, some of whom may be bachelors and others, like him, who are not. As many as a dozen will gang up on a female, chase her, pin her down, and rape her.

White-fronted bee-eater males, for example, may ambush a female that dares to venture from her nesting chamber unaccompanied by her mate. They force her to the ground, where she'll try to protect herself by spreading her tail and pressing it against the ground, making it difficult for her molesters to make sexual contact. Nevertheless, they try, and sometimes several will mount her at the same time.

The average white-fronted bee-eater female is likely to come under this type of attack six or seven times during the week that she is at the peak of egg-laying, according to observations by Dr. Stephen T. Emlen and Dr. Peter H. Wregge. They also noticed that if her mate is in the vicinity and escorts the female from her nest, the bullies rarely bother them. Surprisingly, Emlen and his colleagues found that the attackers in this species were primarily mated males, rather than those without a mate.

Ornithologists have a polite term for this. It's called forced copulation. They can call it what they want; it's still rape. And it occurs in several bird species, including purple martins, bank swallows, gulls and herons, as well as in some ducks.

Mallards are probably the most notorious avian rapists, and are the most likely to be observed, sometimes by genteel strollers on tranquil rambles past the park duck pond. Waterfowl are generally monogamous, yet mallard drakes, whether captive or wild, may try to heighten their chances of successfully fathering offspring by attempting to fertilize other females while their own mates are occupied on the nest.

Typically, a mallard drake – or a group of drakes – takes off in wild pursuit of a hen whose mate is not in attendance at the moment. She does nothing to incite this; in fact, she will do all she can to elude them, flying far, if necessary, and incorporating abrupt twists and turns. Someone who was watching one of these erratic chases saw a hen fly frantically into a wooded area, darting around trees with her pursuers hot on her trail. They were so intent on the chase that one of the drakes wasn't watchful enough about his flight path and went headlong, at full speed, into a tree, killing himself.

If the mallard hen is on water, she'll dive time and again to try to escape her tormentor, and struggle with all her might to break away. If the brute manages to get hold of her, he'll rape her. If there are a number of males, several may jump onto her at once, forcing her underwater. If she's lucky, she won't drown. Afterward, the assailant beats a hasty retreat before the victim's mate comes upon the scene and launches an attack.

Rape is so common among mallards, with enough of the assaults resulting in successful insemination, that multiple paternity can be found in nearly half of the broods hatched in some areas.

Other ducks commit rape, too. Dr. Joe Robb, studying waterfowl at Muscadeck National Wildlife Refuge in central Indiana in mid-May, saw what he estimated to be more than 50, and perhaps as many as 75, drake wood ducks assaulting one hen. The attack, amidst a bubbling mass of birds and water, lasted 20 minutes.

Although rape in birds is sexually motivated (unlike most human rapes), the attacks, nevertheless, are often vicious, and a female may be badly injured, or even killed, particularly if she has been subjected to repeated rape.

Infanticide, the crime of killing young children, is sometimes committed by certain birds, like this barn swallow. Often, the murderer becomes the new mate of the victims' parent and the two produce another brood.

"BOYFRIEND MURDERS WIDOW'S CHILDREN" — INFANTICIDE

There are times when the news is full of headlines that scream, "Mother Kills Her Own Children," "Man Shoots Girlfriend's Son," or "Children Murdered by Stepfather."

Infanticide, the killing of one's own or another's young children, is a shocking crime, all the more so if there are several victims involved. This was the situation when the gruesome remains were discovered one spring morning in a rural barn. The four tiny bodies were found on the barn floor, where they had been dumped. Examination revealed that all had suffered severe blows to the head and body.

Meanwhile, the murderer had moved into the home of their mother, who was recently widowed, and he became her lover.

He, a male barn swallow, couldn't be bothered with helping her raise kids that weren't his, so one morning when she had been out and the children left alone, he paid them a visit and did his dastardly deed. When the female returned, her family had disappeared, and before the day was out, the killer was courting her. Soon they were starting another family, which he would help rear because they would be his offspring.

It has probably been going on for millennia, but infanticide in a monogamous bird species wasn't actually documented until 1984, when Drs. Janice Crooks and William Shield observed several cases of infanticide during their studies of barn swallows.

Since then, it has been found in male and female tree swallows, a male cattle egret, a female little egret, male and female tropical house wrens, female jacanas, and both sexes of house sparrow. In fact, in at least some populations of house sparrows, infanticide, either by egg destruction or killing of chicks, is a major cause of nestling mortality. In the barn swallows that Crook and Shields studied, infanticide was the second leading cause of nestling death.

Apparently it's not because these birds are homicidal maniacs, but because they are trying to increase their reproductive opportunities. In some cases, infanticide is committed by a male in the nest of a widow or deserted female, or sometimes the other way around, as in the jacana. Other times, it happens even though both parents are still alive and together. In these cases, it's not unusual for a divorce to follow the loss of their family, with the murderer taking up with the newly single parent. Usually, the same nest is used, a time-saver which shortens the breeding cycle.

Circumstances varied among the different species and sexes. For example, some female house sparrows turned to murder when they had a nest of young themselves, but were sharing a male with another female. The young of the bigamist's other wife became her victims. The pay-off for her was that the male would not have to divide his paternal responsibilities between her nest and the other.

A male cattle egret that may have thought his injured mate had died or deserted him because she was long overdue from a feeding foray, rolled their single egg out of the nest. That done, he began courtship displays and attracted a new mate within two days. Four days after that, the new wife began her own clutch in the same nest. This was an unusual case, because infanticide by parent birds is rare, but may happen if either resources or breeding opportunities are limited for some reason.

The drastic strategy works in many cases. Often, the perpetrator subsequently mates with the victims' parent.

ALTERNATIVE
LIFESTYLES

*Some female California gulls form lesbian pairs, build nests and lay eggs,
just like heterosexual pairs. A shortage of available breeding males seems to
be forcing the females into lesbian relationships.*

A HERSTORY OF LESBIANISM

In late March, on an island off the California coast, a devoted couple is busy renovating their seasonal home. Like many of their neighbors in this family-oriented colony, they return to the same spot, with the same spouse, year after year. The only difference between this pair and others in the community is that they are among the 8 to 14 percent of the residents that are lesbians.

After building their nest, the pair, two female western gulls, customarily produce twice as many eggs as most of their neighbors, although the eggs are somewhat smaller than normal and often infertile. Still, the twosome do their best to bring off a brood.

They court, and occasionally copulate just like straight couples, and they both lay eggs, which is why they have double-sized clutches. However, they can't fertilize their own eggs . . . nor do they have access to a sperm bank. Often, that's not a problem, because there are always mated males nearby who are willing to have an extra-marital fling and inseminate one or the other, or both. Sperm, after all, is about the only thing lesbian gulls need from males; the rest they can handle themselves.

They tend not to go in for courtship feeding, as male-female pairs do, so their eggs are generally somewhat smaller. The extra nutrients a female receives through the food that a male brings to her are converted into larger eggs that result in a higher survival rate after hatching. In addition, many of their eggs are infertile because not all members of lesbian pairs have promiscuous encounters with unfaithful males. Factors such as these take their toll. Only about 30 to 35 percent of the eggs produced by a female-female pair will hatch, compared to hatching success of about 70 percent for male-female pairs.

However, if any of their eggs do hatch, the two females work together to feed and defend their youngsters just as effectively as other gull parents. Just like straight pairs, while one is away feeding, the other always remains to protect the nest and its contents from marauding neighbors. So, if at least one of them has been fertilized by a male, the couple stands a fair chance of seeing their chicks fledge.

"Some people are born lesbians, some achieve lesbianism, and some have lesbianism thrust upon them," contends writer Helen Eisenbach. In the case of these western gulls, researchers are leaning to the "thrust upon them" explanation to interpret what is aberrant behavior for birds.

In fact, homosexuality had not been reported in wild birds before 1972, when Drs. Molly and George Hunt, Jr. of the University of California, Irvine, discovered it in western gulls nesting on Santa Barbara Island.

Since then, lesbian pairs have also been found in ring-billed, red-billed, herring, and California gulls, as well as in Caspian terns, Canada geese, and at least once in lesser snow geese.

The phenomenon could be the result of a combination of factors that center on a shortage of available breeding males. On Santa Barbara Island, for example, female gulls outnumbered males by about two to one. In addition, contamination from estrogenic chemicals apparently decreased the males' interest in breeding.

DDT and certain other chemicals can mimic the female hormone estrogen. Released into the environment, these substances have a feminizing effect on both males and females, from alligators and sturgeon to birds and mammals, including people.

Estrogenic chemicals can produce exaggerated reproductive organs in females or result in what is, essentially, chemical castration in males. With a shortage of available males that are still interested in breeding, the females have adapted by pairing with one another. " . . . Some have lesbianism thrust upon them."

*Can a gay male bird convince a straight male that he is actually a female?
This hooded warbler male pulled off the illusion flawlessly.*

M. BUTTERFLY:
GAY DECEPTION

About three feet off the ground, in a dense thicket of oak saplings on the side of a ravine, sits a male hooded warbler on a nest that he himself had built. This is peculiar, because it is virtually unheard of for males of this species to participate in nest building, let alone incubation or brooding. But that's not surprising for this individual; he's different in a lot of ways. For starters, he's gay.

It hasn't been easy for him. Not because of any gay bashing or homophobia, which apparently is nonexistent in his society, but because all the guys he meets are pretty straight. He's had to use a little deception, adopting a more feminine manner. It had worked last year, but after their nest had been destroyed, he and his partner separated. His ex was now mated to a female in the same territory they had shared as a couple.

He, on the other hand, was now mated to a male in an adjacent territory. His new partner had been in possession of the tract for three years, and did all the things a macho bird was expected to do. The ravine reverberated with his loud, clear song, he skillfully defended the territory and the nest, and brought food to his incubating mate.

The eggs were a bit of luck. One was quite large, probably laid by a cowbird, but the other was definitely a hooded warbler egg. That was something of a mystery, because the gay male certainly didn't lay it. Perhaps a female that had just lost a nest but still had an egg to lay caught sight of this nest and deposited it there. But as far as his partner knew, these were their very own eggs.

When the youngsters hatched, one a tiny warbler baby and the other a big, bruising cowbird chick, both parents kept busy feeding their family.

The gay warbler's role-playing had worked, enabling him to fulfill his nesting urge.

Although it is seen from time to time in captive birds, there are few examples of true homosexual pairings in wild birds. Male rock doves (pigeons) have been seen mounting each other, and Canada geese, too, have been known to form gay and lesbian pairs.

For the most part, however, male homosexual behavior in wild birds is a case of mistaken identity when males and females of a species look alike. Or, it's a form of aggression, such as when a male, usually the dominant one, mounts another male, often one that has been interfering with courtship activities. Cloacal contact usually isn't made.

There was also a case, though, of homosexual gang rape in tree swallows, in which a group of males chased another male and several managed to copulate with him. There was no obvious explanation for this incident, although it may have been mistaken identity, because plumage of older female tree swallows can closely resemble that of males. What puzzled the researchers was why the victim didn't resist cloacal contact the way a female would, by keeping his tail in the way or by flying off. It's possible that he became submissive in order to avoid being injured by his attackers.

Some female hooded warblers, too, have a lot of black on their heads, and could certainly be mistaken for males based on looks alone. This might make it possible for a male exhibiting female behavior to be treated like a female.

Life in some breeding groups of swamphens is one big love fest, involving various combinations of group members in the sexual escapades. Trysts might be between male-female, male-male, or female-female.

AC/DC

Imagine the identity crisis you might face if you were a large colorful gallinule known as a pukeko, or swamphen, or purple gallinule, bald coot, waterhen, or a half dozen other names, depending on where you were living.

On the other hand, that's not so bad. What's really tough is trying to figure out your family and friends . . . specifically, who's doing what to whom, and what role, if any, you might have in it.

You're living in a group of about 12 individuals. The assemblage consists of a few of your immature brothers, sisters, step-brothers and step-sisters and some adults, including your mom and dad . . . although you're not really certain which ones are really your parents, because everyone helped raise you. Besides, they all look alike, with deep violet-blue head and body, a turquoise gloss on the throat and breast, black upperparts, long, red legs, and a scarlet bill and shield on the front of the head. The younger members of the group are not quite as colorful.

The sexual orientation of your friends and relatives becomes decidedly blurred as you scrutinize the scandalous conduct of your compan-

ions. It's the breeding season, and they're behaving outrageously. Most of the time, the dominant male and female make love to one another, but occasionally he does it with the other adult female, she with another male. Actually, she might have sex with any of the mature males in the group.

But that's not as confusing as when you then see that the dominant male is getting it on with another male. They did this yesterday, too, but that time the other one was on top.

Later, the dominant female mounts the other breeding female and has sex with her. Whew . . . you need a scorecard to keep track of the players in this game!

You eventually realize that you'll have to be ready for anything when you reach maturity. In the meantime, you'll hang around while the adults continue to dally with one another and the two breeding females lay all their eggs in a communal nest. When the next generation breaks into the world, you'll be there to assist in their care and feeding, as is expected.

Eventually, you'll have had enough of them, and they of you, so you'll be on your way, tail flicking flirtatiously, to join another group.

Watch your back.

This may not be everyday behavior for all swamphens, or pukekos, but it has been observed in some groups. When both the males and females of a species are polygamous, as can be the case with swamphens, they are said to be polygynandrous. (Try saying that word quickly three times.)

Perhaps a new word needs to be coined that would describe polygynandry when it is combined with homosexuality. Maybe homo-heteropolygynandry.

A sex change for birds doesn't require surgery. In one case, a mother hen gradually changed into a virile rooster and eventually became a father.

GLEN OR GLENDA?

When someone feels that he is a woman trapped in a man's body, or vice versa, he or she may elect to have a sex change operation.

In birds, gender change, usually from female to male, occasionally occurs whether or not the individual is in favor of it. Unlike humans, they don't have to go under the knife; it's a completely noninvasive procedure.

The most bizarre and extreme example may be the farmyard hen that had been a prolific layer and the classic mother hen to a number of chicks until she was about three and a half years old.

Then, one morning, she started to crow. One couldn't help but notice that she was looking and behaving increasingly like a rooster, eventually sporting wattles and hackle feathers and strutting like the best of them.

About a year later, the onetime female became a father after copulating with a young hen that subsequently presented R.F.K.A.H. (the Rooster Formerly Known as Hen) with two chicks.

After R.F.K.A.H. died, a postmortem revealed that it had two testes in working order. On its left side was a shriveled ovary, perhaps due to a tumor.

R.F.K.A.H.'s case is well documented because the bird lived in an environment in which it was easy to monitor the transformation, but sex changes occur in wild birds, too.

Female birds have an ovary on each side, but only the left one is functional in most species. If that ovary stops working for some reason, the right one may kick in and became an ovitestis, secreting male, rather than female, hormones. If that happens, the bird develops male plumage and behavior.

Changes such as these have been recorded in pheasants, partridges, ducks, herons, ostriches, chaffinches, European robins, rufous-sided towhees and others.

So far, there don't seem to be any reports of transsexual wild birds that have produced viable sperm and sired chicks. Still, if R.F.K.A.H. could do it, anything is possible.

No long-term commitments, no domestic responsibilities, just uncomplicated sex. The down side is that this lifestyle translates to few surviving offspring. For many ostriches, that's the way the mating game is played. Most never manage to achieve the stability of a permanent relationship.

FREE LOVE

The equatorial sun was easing toward the horizon when the two first met. He had been patrolling the western end of his territorial holdings, and she had wandered in not knowing whose land she was entering.

They were attracted immediately, and one thing soon led to another. Before long, she impetuously threw herself on the ground and there they satisfied their lust.

He wasn't counting, but she must have been the third or fourth he had seduced that day, even though he was committed to another. For her part, it didn't seem to bother her that he was attached, or that she hadn't been his first and only conquest today. In fact, earlier in the day, she had given herself to a handsome but homeless bachelor.

Their behavior was not shocking, considering they were ostriches. Ostrich society, after all, advocates free love.

She had been temporarily living with other unmated ostriches in a group of varying size as members came and went. It was a great place for singles to meet, but probably wouldn't lead to any permanent relationship. For that, she'd need to find a territory-holding male that was looking for a long-term mate, and only one out of three females managed to achieve that.

The mature and experienced male that the ostrich hen just encountered had courted her skillfully, alternately raising his plumed right wing and then the left. He dropped to the ground, swaying his head, then jumped up again. That's when she flopped down, allowing him to mount her.

Recently, he had used his strong feet to scrape out a nest in a sandy spot near the center of his territory, and his mate of many years, the major hen, had laid her first egg three days ago. She would add another egg every second day until she had laid about seven.

In the meantime, the liberal-minded pair would allow other females – minor hens such as the one who had just entered their territory – to lay eggs in the nest. By the time the clutch is complete, in about two weeks, the communal nest could hold up to 70 eggs from more than 15 hens, although 40 eggs from 10 hens is average.

Minor hens roam over expansive home territories and breed with many males over the course of the breeding season. At the same time, the males, whether unmated or permanently paired, court and copulate with a number of females.

Because minor hens have no nest of their own, they are obliged to leave their eggs of dubious parentage in the communal nests of established pairs, who are as accepting of them as if they were benevolently running an orphanage.

All eggs are not equal in the eyes of the major hen, however. She is able to recognize her own eggs and favors them by keeping them in the center of the nest. An ostrich can only cover about 20 of the eggs while incubating, so the surplus eggs, often rolled to the rim or outside of the nest, never hatch.

All the breeding birds get something out of this arrangement. The major hen finds safety in numbers for her eggs. If a predator raids the nest, it would first take the eggs easiest to nab, those on the perimeter, rather than hers in the center.

The resident male benefits by raising his reproductive rate through the minor hens contributing to his nest. Some of the eggs will have been sired by other males, but enough of them should be his to make it worthwhile.

The unmated males and the minor hens benefit because they get to breed and may have one or more of their chicks hatched and raised by adoptive parents.

When all the eggs have been laid, the minor hens are usually no longer allowed access to the nest. The responsibility of incubation is taken on by the more stable pair, with the male taking the longer overnight shift.

Polygynandry — males mating with multiple females and vice versa — happens regularly in only a few bird species. In South America, the greater rhea male competes to acquire a harem of up to 15 females with whom he mates. He builds a nest, entices them to lay their eggs in it, then drives them off. He incubates the eggs and looks after the chicks when they hatch. The bevy of females, meanwhile, go cruising for another male. Over the course of the season, they may mate with as many as seven males, staying with each one just long enough to fill his nest with 20 to 50 eggs.

Polygynandry is also reported occasionally in other species where it is not their primary mating system but does occur. It apparently happens regularly in alpine accentors. And in Smith's longspur's, most of the females mate with two or three males who are at the same time mated to two or three females.

Acorn woodpeckers live in true commune style, with all members partici-pating in the feeding and rearing of the next generation.

HIPPIE COMMUNES

Hey man, I brought this really groovy dragonfly for the kids, but wow . . . like it might be too big for them," the young acorn woodpecker seems to be chattering as he pauses, bewildered, at the entrance to his commune's nest chamber.

One of the adults from the clan, a female that has just fed one of the nestlings, is clinging to the bark just inches away from him. Recognizing his inexperience in these matters, she gets him to pass the insect to her. She takes it to a horizontal branch just below them, promptly removes the insect's wings, pummels it to soften it up a bit, returns to the entrance hole and stuffs it into the mouth of one of the hungry youngsters.

The teenager has been trying to help, but now it looks like he thinks it's all too much hard work. He flits away, perhaps yearning for the days, not long ago, when he was the one being served.

Meanwhile, two more members of the commune approach with food, and a clamor arises within the cavity of the white oak as the nestlings boisterously anticipate another delivery.

The juvenile acorn woodpecker is one of twelve in his group, including the five nestlings who are his younger siblings. They're just one big happy family, sharing everything. Even the two couples who produced the eggs from which the latest generation of chicks hatched sometimes share more of themselves than their mates might like, if they knew about it. Maybe they do know, but are themselves sneaking occasional adulterous interludes within the group.

When it came time to nest, the two breeding females both laid eggs in the same nest. Of course, when left alone with the eggs, one female might destroy an egg or two belonging to the other, even if it was her sister's. Normally, over a third of the eggs laid in a communal acorn woodpecker nest are destroyed this way. The girls just lay a few more to try to compensate.

Generally, however, there is peace in the group and they live in contented harmony. For example, as soon as the egg-laying was finished, everyone took turns incubating. In fact, they were all so eager to do their share that, at times, the average shift was little more than five minutes during the daytime.

Now that there were noisy youngsters demanding to be fed, all able-bodied group members were equally willing to provide nourishment for them and to help rear them for some time after they have fledge, regardless of what blood tests might reveal about the young ones' parentage.

In the winter, they'll share their caches of acorns with each other, and will probably all huddle together in one or two roosting cavities, a cozy, tightly-knit, extended family.

Acorn woodpeckers may live in pairs, or in groups of as many as 15 individuals. They reside with one another throughout the year, in true commune style, sharing a joint nest during the breeding season, with all members participating in raising the young and storing acorns for the winter. Depending on the group and the resources available in their habitat, the breeding adults may be monogamous, polygynous, polyandrous, or polygynandrous.

The smooth-billed ani and groove-billed ani, both members of the cuckoo family, engage in a variation of this theme. Several pairs may join together to participate in building a loosely constructed twig nest lined with fresh green leaves into which all the females lay eggs. One smooth-billed ani nest that belonged to a group of 15 contained 29 eggs. The most that have been found in a groove-billed ani nest were 20 eggs contributed by 5 females. Unlike an acorn woodpecker commune, which often includes immatures and non-breeding helpers, an ani nesting flock only consists of breeding pairs.

Numerous other species, among them bluebirds and swallows, are assisted by non-breeding helpers during the nesting cycle, usually offspring from a previous brood. These typically revolve around a single breeding pair.

GLOSSARY

Brood: Noun: The offspring from a single nest. Verb: To provide warmth and protection to nestlings, and in some cases to fledglings, by covering them with the body or wings.

Cloaca: In birds, the passage through which feces and urine, as well as sperm from males and eggs from females, are discharged.

Clutch: The eggs in a single nesting.

Conspecific: Belonging to the same species.

Cooperative Breeding: A breeding system in which birds other than the chicks' mother and father assist in caring for the young.

Cooperative Courtship: Two or more males working in harmony to court a female for the benefit of just one of the males.

Copulation: Sexual coupling. In birds, it is accomplished by the male and female pressing their cloacas together.

Cuckoldry: In birds, a male's involuntary rearing of another male's offspring as a result of extra-pair copulation.

Cygnet: The young of a swan.

DNA Fingerprinting: A technique used to establish certainty of maternity and paternity.

Extra-Pair Copulation: Adultery.

False Mating: Masturbation.

Family: In bird classifications, Family is next in line under the category Order. Each family consists of one or more genera.

Fecal Sac: A sac containing excrement that is expelled by baby birds, making it easy for the adult birds to remove it from the nest to maintain sanitation.

Floater: A bird with no mate, nest or territory that nevertheless may try to breed.

Forced Copulation: Rape.

Genera: Plural of genus.

Genus: In classifying birds, Genus falls under the category Family. Each genus contains one or more species.

Gonads: Testes in males; ovaries in females.

Incubation: Keeping eggs at a constant, warm temperature until they

hatch. Birds, with very few exceptions, do this by warming the eggs with their own body heat.

Infanticide: In birds, the destruction of eggs or killing of young.

Interspecific: Between different species.

Lek: An area that is used exclusively for courtship displays. Depending on the species, it may also be called a booming ground, strutting ground, dancing ground, or arena.

Mate Guarding: Maintaining close contact with a mate during the fertile period as a means of preventing illegitimate offspring.

Mixed Reproductive Strategy: Employing more than one tactic to increase reproduction; e.g., monogamy along with adultery.

Monogamy: One male mated to one female. In general, however, monogamy in birds does not preclude adultery.

Order: One of the higher categories in bird classifications. It is below Class (Aves), and each order includes one or more families.

Oviduct: The passage through which an egg passes from the ovary to the cloaca.

Ovitestis: An ovary that develops into a testis.

Polyandry: Polygamy by females.

Polygamy: Having multiple mates, sequentially or simultaneously.

Polygynandry: A mating system in which both males and females are polygamous.

Polygyny: Polygamy by males.

Sexual Dimorphism: A difference in outward appearance between male and female birds, usually by a distinction in plumage.

Territory: A habitat defended by a single bird, pair, or breeding group.

Vole: Any of various small burrowing rodents which include the meadow mouse in America, and the field mouse in Europe.

BIBLIOGRAPHY

Altmann, Stuart A. et al. Two models for the evolution of polygyny. *Behavioral Ecology and Sociobiology,* vol. 2, 1977, p. 397-410.

Alvarez del Toro, Miguel. On the biology of the American finfoot in southern Mexico. *Living Bird,* vol. 10, 1971, p. 79-88.

Armstrong, Edward A. Dances of birds and men. *Discovery,* Jul. 1943, p. 215-218.

Bailey, Robert O. et al. Rape behavior in blue-winged teal. *Auk,* vol. 95, Jan. 1978, p. 188-190.

Barash, David P. Rape among mallards. *Science,* vol. 201, Jul. 21, 1978, p. 282.

Barash, David P. Sociobiology of rape in mallards Anas platyrhynchos; response of the mated male. *Science,* vol. 197, Aug. 19, 1977, p. 788-789.

Bateson, Patrick. Preferences for cousins in Japanese quail. *Nature,* vol. 295, Jan. 21, 1982, p. 236-237.

Bednarz, James C. Pair and group reproductive success, polyandry, and cooperative breeding in Harris' hawks. *Auk,* vol. 104, no. 3, Jul. 1987, p. 393-404.

Beehler, Bruce. Frugivory and polygamy in birds of paradise. *Auk,* vol. 100, no. 1, Jan. 1983, p. 1-12.

Beehler, Bruce. Lek behavior of the lesser bird of paradise. *Auk,* vol. 100, no. 4, Oct. 1983, p. 992-995.

Beletsky, Les D. et al. Steroid hormones in relation to territoriality, breeding density, and parental behavior in male yellow-headed blackbirds. *Auk,* vol. 108, no. 1, Jan. 1990, p. 60-68.

Bent, Arthur Cleveland. *Life Histories of North American Blackbirds, Orioles, Tanagers, and Allies.* Dover Publications, Inc., New York, 1965.

Bent, Arthur Cleveland. *Life Histories of North American Shore Birds, Part One.* Dover Publications, Inc., New York, 1962.

Bent, Arthur Cleveland. *Life Histories of North American Shore Birds, Part Two.* Dover Publications, Inc., New York, 1962.

Bent, Arthur Cleveland. *Life Histories of North American Woodpeckers.* Dover Publications, Inc., New York, 1964.

Berger, Cynthia. Cuckoldry: For male starlings it's worth brooding about. *Living Bird Quarterly,* vol. 9, no. 2, Spring 1990, p. 26.

Birkhead, Tim R. and Anders P. Møller. Avian mating games. *New Scientist,* vol. 112, Dec. 18, 1986, p. 34-36.

Birkhead, Tim and Anders P. Møller. Faithless female seeks better genes . . . *New Scientist,* vol. 135, Jul. 4, 1992, p. 34-38.

Birkhead, Tim R. and Anders P. Møller. Avian mating games. *New Scientist,* Dec. 18, 1986, p. 35-36.

Birkhead, Tim R. and Anders P. Møller. Female control of paternity. *Tree,* vol. 8, no. 3, Mar. 1993, p. 100-104.

Birkhead, Tim R. and Anders P. Møller. Old sperm but good sperm. *New Scientist,* Dec. 18, 1986, p. 35.

Birkhead, Tim R. and Anders P. Møller. Why do male birds stop copulating while their partners are still fertile? *Animal Behaviour,* vol. 45, 1993, p. 105-118.

Birkhead, Tim R. and C.M. Lessells. Copulation behaviour of the osprey Pandion haliaetus. *Animal Behaviour,* vol. 36, Nov./Dec. 1988, p. 1672-1682.

Birkhead, Tim R. et al. Extra-pair copulation and sperm competition in the zebra finch. *Nature,* vol. 354, Jul. 7, 1988, p. 60-62.

Birkhead, Tim R. Mate guarding in the magpie Pica pica. *Animal Behaviour,* vol. 27, no. 3, 1979, p. 866-874.

Björklund, Mats et al. Female great tits, *Parus major,* avoid extra-pair copulation attempts. *Animal Behaviour,* vol. 43, Apr. 1992, p. 691-693.

Blakey, Jeremy K. and Ken Norris. Do female great tits avoid extra-pair copulations? A comment on Björklund et al. *Animal Behaviour,* vol. 47, May 1994, p. 1227-1229.

Blakey, Jeremy K. Genetic evidence for extra-pair fertilizations in a monogamous passerine, the Great Tit *Parus major. Ibis,* vol. 136, Oct. 1994, p. 457-462.

Bowen, Bonnie S. et al. Seasonal pattern of reverse mounting in the groove-billed ani *(Crotophaga sulcirostris). Condor,* vol. 93, Feb. 1991, p. 159-163.

Boxer, S. Why the old alibi just won't fly for these unfaithful penguins. *Discover,* vol. 8, Jan. 1987, p. 13.

Brewer, Gwen. Courtship of ducklings by adult male Chiloe wigeon *(Anas sibilatrix). Auk,* vol. 108, Oct. 1991, p. 969-973.

Briskie, James V. Anatomical adaptations to sperm competition in Smith's longspurs and other polygynandrous passerines. *Auk,* vol. 110, no. 4, Oct. 1993, p. 875-888.

Briskie, James V. Copulation patterns and sperm competition in the polygynandrous Smith's longspur. *Auk*, vol. 109, no. 3, Jul. 1992, p. 563-575.

Briskie, James V. Lack of sperm storage by female migrants and the significance of copulation en route. *Condor*, vol. 98, May 1996, p. 414-417.

Brooke, M. de L. and N. B. Davies. Egg mimicry by cuckoos *Cuculus canorus* in relation to discrimination by hosts. *Nature*, vol. 335, Oct. 13, 1988, p. 630-632.

Brooke, Michael. Tricks of the egg trade. *Natural History*, Apr., 1989, p. 50-54.

Brooke, Michaél. The devious means by which some birds sire offspring. *New Scientist*, vol. 135, Sep. 19, 1992, p. 16.

Brown, Charles R. Laying eggs in a neighbor's nest: benefit and cost of colonial nesting in swallows. *Science*, vol. 224, May 4, 1984, p. 518-519.

Brown, Charles. R. and Mary Bomberger Brown. A new form of reproductive parasitism in cliff swallows. *Nature*, vol. 331, Jan. 7, 1988, p. 66-68.

Bruce, Jeffrey P. et al. DNA fingerprinting reveals monogamy in the bushtit, a cooperatively breeding species. *Auk*, vol. 113, Apr. 1996, p. 511-516.

Burke, T. et al. Parental care and mating behaviour of polyandrous dunnocks *Prunella modularis* related to paternity by DNA fingerprinting. *Nature*, vol. 338, Mar. 16, 1989, p. 249-251.

Carey, Michael and Val Nolan. Polygyny in indigo buntings: A hypothesis tested. *Science*, vol. 190, Dec. 26, 1975, p. 1296-1297.

Castro, I. et al. Polygynandry, face-to-face copulation and sperm competition in the Hihi Notiohystis cincta *(Aves: Meliphagidae)*. *Ibis*, vol. 138, 1996, p. 765-771.

Catchpole, Clive. Deceit among the songbirds. *New Scientist*, Apr. 17, 1986, p. 45-47.

Cezilly, Frank and Ruedi G. Nager. Comparative evidence for a positive association between divorce and extra-pair paternity in birds. *The Proceedings of the Royal Society*, London, 1995. 262, p. 7-12.

Chek, Andrew A. and Raleigh J. Robertson. Infanticide in female tree swallows: A role for sexual selection. *Condor*, vol. 93, May 1991, p. 454-457.

Cheke, A.S. Copulation in the hammerkop *Scopus umbretta*. Ibis, vol. 110, 1968, p. 201-203.

Cherfas, Jeremy. Crime pays for male bowerbirds. *New Scientist*, vol. 111, Jul. 10, 1986, p. 33.

Choudhury, Sharmila. Divorce in birds: a review of the hypotheses. *Animal Behaviour*, vol. 50, 1995, p. 413-429.

Clotfelter, Ethan D. Courtship displaying and intrasexual competition in the bronzed cowbird. *Condor*, vol. 97, Aug. 1995, p. 816-818.

Clutton-Brock, T.H. and A.D.J. Vincent. Sexual selection and the potential reproductive rates of males and females. *Nature*, vol. 351, May 2, 1991, p. 58-60.

Colburn, Thea et al. *Our Stolen Future*. Dutton, New York, 1996.

Collias, Nicholas E. and Elsie C. Collias. *Nest Building and Bird Behavior*. Princeton University Press, Princeton, 1984.

Colwell, Mark A. The first documented case of polyandry for Wilson's phalarope *(Phalaropus tricolor)*. *Auk*, vol. 103, no. 3, Jul. 1986, p. 611-612.

Conover, Michael R. and Hunt, George L., Jr. Female-female pairing and sex ratios in gulls: an historical perspective. *Wilson Bulletin*, vol. 96, no. 4, Dec. 1984, p. 619-625.

Cooke, F. et al. Assortative mating in lesser snow geese (Anser caerulescens). *Behavior Genetics*, vol. 6, no. 2, 1976, p. 127-139.

Cooke, F. et al. Mate change and reproductive success in the lesser snow goose. *Condor*, vol. 83, 1981, p. 322-327.

Cox, Cathleen R. and Burney J. Le Boeuf. Female incitation of male competition: A mechanism in sexual selection. *American Naturalist*, vol. 111, no. 978, Mar./Apr. 1977, p. 317-335.

Craig, John L. and Ian G. Jamieson. Incestuous mating in a communal bird: a family affair. *American Naturalist*, vol. 131, no. 1, Jan. 1988, p. 58-70.

Crook, Janice R. and W.M. Shields. Sexually selected infanticide by adult male barn swallows. *Animal Behaviour*, vol. 33, 1985, p. 754-761.

Crook, Janice R. Barn swallow social behavior: Nest attendance, aggression, sexually selected infanticide. Thesis. Oxford University, Oxford, 1984.

Davies, N.B. Polyandry, cloaca-pecking and sperm competition in dunnocks. *Nature*, vol. 302, Mar. 24, 1983, p. 334-336.

Davies, Nicholas B. and Michael Brooke. Coevolution of the cuckoo and its hosts. *Scientific American*, Jan. 1991, p. 92-98.

Davies, Nicholas B. Dumping eggs on conspecifics. *Nature*, vol. 331, Jan. 7, 1988, p. 19.

Dawkins, R. and T.R. Carlisle. Parental investment,

mate desertion and a fallacy. *Nature,* vol. 262, Jul. 8, 1976, p. 131-132.

Dawson, James W. and R. William Mannan. Dominance hierarchies and helper contributions in Harris' hawks. *Auk,* vol. 108, Jul. 1991, p. 649-659.

Diamond, Jared M. A Darwinian theory of divorce. *Nature,* vol. 329, Oct. 29, 1987, p. 765-766.

Diamond, Jared M. Borrowed sexual ornaments. *Nature,* vol. 349, Jan. 10, 1991, p. 105.

Diamond, Jared M. Goslings of gay geese. *Nature,* vol. 340, Jul. 13, 1989, p. 101.

Dossenbach, Hans D. *The Family Life of Birds.* McGraw-Hill Publishing Company, Maidenhead. 1971.

Droge, Dale L. et al. Sex-biased provisioning: a test for differences in field metabolic rates of nestling eastern bluebirds. *Condor,* vol. 93, no. 4, Nov. 1991, p. 793-798.

Dunn, Peter O. and Raleigh J. Robertson. Extra-pair paternity in polygynous tree swallows. *Animal Behaviour,* vol. 45, 1993, p. 231-239.

Ehrlich, Paul R. et al. *The Birder's Handbook: A Field Guide to the Natural History of North American Birds.* Simon & Schuster/Fireside, New York, 1988.

Emlen, Stephen T. and Natalie J. Demong. All in the family. *Living Bird,* vol. 15, no. 3, Summer 1996, p. 30-34.

Emlen, Stephen T. and Peter H. Wrege. Forced copulations and intra-specific parasitism: two costs of social living in the white-fronted bee-eater. *Ethology,* vol. 71, 1986, p. 2-29.

Emlen, Stephen T. and Peter H. Wrege. Gender, status and family fortunes in the white-fronted bee-eater. *Nature,* vol. 367, Jan. 13, 1994, p. 129-132.

Emlen, Stephen T. et al. Experimental induction of infanticide in female wattled jacanas. *Auk,* vol. 106, no. 1, Jan. 1989, p. 1-7.

Emlen, Stephen T. Living with relatives: lessons from avian family systems. *Ibis,* vol. 138, 1996, p. 87-100.

Evarts, Susan and Christopher J. Williams. Multiple paternity in a wild population of mallards. *Auk,* vol. 104, no. 4, Oct. 1987, p. 597-602.

Faaborg, John and Cindy B. Patterson. The characteristics and occurrence of cooperative polyandry. *Ibis,* vol. 123, 1981, p. 477+.

Faaborg, John et al. Preliminary observations on the occurrence and evolution of polyandry in the Galapagos hawk *(Buteo galapagoensis). Auk,* vol.

97, Jul. 1980, p. 581-590.

Faaborg, John. Why share a mate? *Living Bird Quarterly,* vol. 2, no. 2, p. 14-17.

Fackelmann, Kathy A. Avian altruism. *Science News,* vol. 135, Jun. 10, 1989, p. 364-365.

Farner, Donald S., ed. *Breeding Biology of Birds.* National Academy of Sciences, Washington, D.C., 1973.

Ficken, Millicent S. and William C. Dilger. Comments on redirection with examples of avian copulations with substitute objects. *Animal Behaviour,* vol. 8, 3-4, Jul.-Oct. 1960, p. 219-222

Fitter, Richard, ed. *Book of British Birds.* Reader's Digest Association, Ltd., London, 1973.

Flood, Nancy J. Incidences of polygyny and extra-pair copulation in the northern oriole. *Auk,* vol. 102, no. 2, Apr. 1995, p. 410-413.

Foster, Mercedes S. Odd couples in manakins: A study of social organization and cooperative breeding in *Chiroxiphia linearis. American Naturalist,* vol. 111, no 981, Sept./Oct. 1977, p. 845-853.

Fretwell, Steve. Is the lady a tramp? *Bird Watch,* vol. 5, no. 8, Oct. 1977, p. 1-3.

Frith, Dawn and Clifford. Say it with bowers. *Wildlife Conservation,* vol. 94, no. 1, Jan./Feb. 1991, p. 74-83.

Fujioka, Masahiro. Infanticide by a male parent and by a new female mate in colonial egrets. *Auk,* vol. 103, no. 3, Jul. 1986, p. 619-621.

Gavin, Thomas A. and Eric K. Bollinger. Multiple paternity in a territorial passerine: the bobolink. *Auk,* vol. 102, no. 3, Jul. 1985, p. 550-555.

Gibbs, H. Lisle et al. Realized reproductive success of polygynous red-winged blackbirds revealed by DNA markers. *Science,* vol. 250, Dec. 7, 1990, p. 1394-1396.

Gjershaug, J.O. et al. Marriage entrapment by "solitary" mothers: a study on male deception by female pied flycatchers. *American Naturalist,* vol. 133, no. 2, Feb. 1989, p. 273-276.

Gladstone, Douglas E. Promiscuity in monogamous colonial birds. *American Naturalist,* vol. 114, no. 4, Oct. 1979, p. 545-557.

Glue, David. A host of cuckoos. *Birds,* vol. 11, no. 2, Summer 1986, p. 46-51.

Graham, Donald S. Rejection, desertion, burial, and the wanton layers. *Living Bird Quarterly,* Spring 1989, vol. 8, no. 2, p. 21-24.

Grant, Peter R. and B. Rosemary Grant. Hybridization of bird species. *Science,* vol. 256, Apr. 10,

1992, p. 193-197.

Gyllensten, Ulf B. et al. No evidence for illegitimate young in monogamous and polygynous warblers. *Nature,* vol. 343, Jan. 11, 1990, p. 168-170.

Hailman, Jack P. Rape among mallards. *Science,* vol. 201, Jul. 21, 1978, p. 280-281.

Harrison, Hal H. *A Field Guide to Western Birds' Nests.* Houghton Mifflin Company, Boston, 1979.

Harrison, Kit. The Galapagos are the real fantasy islands. *Exclusively Yours,* May 1979, p. 85-89.

Harrison, Kit. Tympanuchus cupido pinnatus—A Wisconsin success story. *Exclusively Yours,* Mar. 1979, p. 79+.

Harvey, Paul H. and David S. Wilcove. Sex among the dunnocks. *Nature,* vol. 313, Jan. 17, 1985, p. 180.

Harvey, Paul H. and Linda Partridge. Of cuckoo clocks and cowbirds. *Nature,* vol. 335, Oct. 13, 1988, p. 586-587.

Heredia, Rafael and Anthony Luke. Ménage à trois for Spain's vultures. *New Scientist,* vol. 128, Dec. 15, 1990, p. 45-47.

Hinde, R.A. The conflict between drives in the courtship and copulation of the chaffinch. *Behaviour,* vol. V, no. 1, 1953, p. 1-31.

Hinde, R.A. The courtship and copulation of the greenfinch *(Chloris chloris). Behaviour,* vol. VII, nos. 2-3, 1955, p. 207-233.

Hitchcock, Ronald R. and Mirarchi, Ralph E. Comparisons between single-parent and normal mourning dove nestings during the post-fledging period. *Wilson Bulletin,* vol. 96, no. 3, Sept. 1984, p. 494-495.

Hoffenberg, Ann S. et al. The frequency of cuckoldry in the European starling *(Sturnus vulgaris). Wilson Bulletin,* vol. 100, Mar. 1988, p. 60-69.

Holley, A.J.F. Naturally arising adoption in the herring gull. *Animal Behaviour,* vol. 29, no. 1, Feb. 1981, p. 302-303.

Howlett, Rory. Sexual selection by female choice in monogamous birds. *Nature,* vol. 332, Apr. 14, 1988, p. 583-584.

Hoyo, Josep del et al, ed. *Handbook of the Birds of the World,* vol. 1, 2 and 3. Lynx Edicions, Barcelona, 1992.

Hunt, George L., Jr. and Molly Warner Hunt. Female-female pairing in western gulls *(Larus occidentalis)* in southern California. *Science,* vol. 196, Jun. 24, 1977, p. 1466-1477.

Hurly, T. Andrew and Raleigh J. Robertson. Do female red-winged blackbirds limit harem size? A removal experiment. *Auk,* vol. 102, no. 1, Jan. 1985, p. 205-209.

Huxley, Julian. Bird-watching and biological science. *Auk,* vol. 33, 1916, p. 142-161.

James, Paul C. Reverse mounting in the northwestern crow. *Journal of Field Ornithology,* vol. 54, no. 4, Autumn 1983, p. 418-419.

Jamieson, Ian G. and Craig, John L. Male-male and female-female courtship and copulation behaviour in a communally breeding bird. *Animal Behaviour,* vol. 35, no. 4, Aug. 1987, p. 1251-1253.

Jenni, Donald A. Evolution of polyandry in birds. *American Zoology,* vol. 14, 1974, p. 129-144.

Jenni, Donald A. Female chauvinist birds. *New Scientist,* Jun. 14, 1979, p. 896-899.

Jenni, Donald A. and Gerald Collier. Polyandry in the American jaçana *(Jacana spinosa). Auk,* vol. 89, Oct. 1972, p. 743-765.

Johnsgard, Paul A. *Waterfowl of North America.* Indiana University Press, Bloomington, 1975.

Kålås, John Atle and Ingvar Byrkjedal. Breeding chronology and mating system of the Eurasian dotterel *(Charadrius morinellus). Auk,* vol. 101, no. 4, Oct. 1984, p. 838-847.

Kemp, Alan C. A review of the hornbills: biology and radiation. *The Living Bird, Seventeenth Annual of the Cornell Laboratory of Ornithology,* Douglas A. Lancaster, ed., 1978, p. 105-136.

Kempenaers, Bart and André A. Dhondt. Why do females engage in extra-pair copulations? A review of hypotheses and their predictions. *Belgian Journal of Zoology,* vol. 123, 1993, p. 93-103.

Kempenaers, Bart et al. Extra-pair paternity results from female preference for high-quality males in the blue tit. *Nature,* vol. 357, Jun. 11, 1992, p. 494-496.

Kilham, Lawrence. Intra- and extrapair copulatory behavior of American crows. *Wilson Bulletin,* vol. 96, no. 4, Dec. 1984, p. 716-717.

Kirkpatrick, Mark and Michael J. Ryan. The evolution of mating preferences and the paradox of the lek. *Nature,* vol. 350, Mar. 7, 1991, p. 33-38.

Klein, Nedra K. and Kenneth V. Rosenberg. Feeding of brown-headed cowbird *(Molothrus ater)* fledglings by more than one "host" species. *Auk,* vol. 103, no. 1, Jan. 1986, p. 213.

Koenig, W.D. et al. Patterns and consequences of egg destruction among joint-nesting acorn woodpeckers. *Animal Behaviour,* vol. 50, no. 3, Sept.,

1995, p. 607-621.

Kovacs, Kit M. and John P. Ryder. Morphology and physiology of female-female pair members. *Auk,* vol 102, no. 4, Oct. 1985, p. 874-878.

Lagrenade, Marie-Christine and Pierre Mousseau. Female-female pairs and polygynous associations in a Québec ring-billed gull colony. *Auk,* vol. 100, no. 1, Jan. 1983, p. 210-212.

Leahy, Christopher. *The Birdwatcher's Companion: An Encyclopedic Handbook of North American Birdlife.* Hill and Wang, New York, 1982.

Lewin, Roger. Hotshots, hotspots, and female preference. *Science,* vol. 240, Jun. 3, 1988, p. 1277-1278.

Lewin, Roger. Judging paternity in the hedge sparrow's world. *Science,* vol. 243, Mar. 31, 1989, p. 1663-1664.

Lifjeld, J.T. et al. Extra-pair paternity in monogamous tree swallows. *Animal Behaviour,* vol. 45, Feb. 1993, p. 213-229.

Lifjeld, Jan T. and Raleigh J. Robertson. Female control of extra-pair fertilization in tree swallows. *Behavioral Ecology and Sociobiology,* vol. 31, 1992, p. 89-96.

Ligon, J. David and Peter B. Stacey. On the significance of helping behavior in birds. *Auk,* vol. 106, Oct. 1989, p. 700-705.

Logan, Cheryl A. Mate switching and mate choice in female northern mockingbirds: facultative monogamy. *Wilson Bulletin,* vol. 103, no. 2, Jun. 2, 1991, p. 277-281.

Lombardo, Michael P. et al. Homosexual copulations by male tree swallows. *Wilson Bulletin,* vol. 106, no. 3, 1994, p. 555-557.

Lotem, Arnon. Learning to recognize nestlings is maladaptive for cuckoo *Cuculus canorus* hosts. *Nature,* vol. 362, Apr. 22, 1993, p. 743-745.

Lucking, Robert S. Polygyny in the Seychelles sunbird *Nectarinia dussumieri*. *Bulletin of the British Ornithologists' Club,* vol. 116, no. 3, 1996, p. 178-179.

Lumpkin, Susan. Avoidance of cuckoldry in birds: the role of the female. *Animal Behaviour,* vol. 29, Feb. 1981, p. 303-304.

Mader, William J. Biology of the Harris' hawk in southern Arizona. *The Living Bird, Fourteenth Annual of the Cornell Laboratory of Ornithology,* Douglas A. Lancaster, ed., 1975, p. 59-85.

Marini, Miguel Ângelo and Robert Brandão Cavalcanti. Mating system of the helmeted manakin *(Antilophila galeata)* in central Brazil. *Auk,* vol. 109, no. 4, Oct. 1992, p. 911-913.

Marra, Peter P. Reverse mounting in the black-throated blue warbler. *Wilson Bulletin,* vol. 105, no. 2, 1993, p. 359-361.

Marshall, A.J. Bower-birds. *Endeavor,* vol. XIX, no. 76, Oct. 1960, p. 202-208.

Martin, Stephen G. Adaptations for polygynous breeding in the bobolink, *Dolichonyx oryzivorus*. *American Zoology,* vol. 14, 1974, p. 109-119.

Masatomi, Hiroyuki. Pseudomale behaviour in a female bengalee. *Journal of the Faculty of Science,* Hokkaido University, Series VI, Zoology, Vol. 13, Nos. 1-4, 1957, p. 187-191.

Mayfield, Harold. Red phalaropes breeding on Bathurst Island. *The Living Bird, Seventeenth Annual of the Cornell Laboratory of Ornithology,* Douglas A. Lancaster, ed., 1978, p. 7-39

Maynard Smith, J. and M.G. Ridpath. Wife sharing in the Tasmanian native hen, Tribonyx mortierii: A case of kin Selection? *American Naturalist,* vol. 106, no. 950, Jul./Aug. 1972, p. 447-452.

McCaffery, Brian J. Breeding flight display in the female white-rumped sandpiper *(Calidris fuscicollis)*. *Auk,* vol. 100, Apr. 1983, p. 500-501.

McDonald, David B. and Wayne K. Potts. Cooperative display and relatedness among males in a lek-mating bird. *Science,* vol. 266, Nov. 11, 1994, p. 1030-1031.

Moksnes, Arne and Røskaft, Eivin. Egg-morphs and host preference in the common cuckoo *(Cuculus canorus)*: an analysis of cuckoo and host eggs from European museum collections. *Journal of Zoology,* vol. 236, Aug. 1995, p. 625-648.

Møller, Anders P. Copulation behaviour in the goshawk, *Accipiter gentilis*. *Animal Behaviour,* vol. 35, Jun. 1987, p. 755-763.

Møller, Anders P. Viability costs of male tail ornaments in a swallow. *Nature,* vol. 339, May 11, 1989, p. 132-135.

Møller, Anders P. and Tim R. Birkhead. Cuckoldry and sociality: a comparative study of birds. *American Naturalist,* vol. 142, no 1, Jul. 1993, p. 118-140.

Møller, Anders P. and Tim R. Birkhead. Frequent copulations and mate guarding as alternative paternity guards in birds: a comparative study. *Behaviour,* vol. VI, 1991, p. 170-186.

Morris, Desmond. The causation of pseudofemale and pseudomale behaviour: a further comment. *Behaviour,* vol. 8, no. 1, 1955, p. 46-55

Morris, Desmond. The reproductive behaviour of the zebra finch *(Poephila guttata)* with special reference to pseudofemale behaviour and displacement activities. *Behaviour,* vol. 6, no. 4, 1954, p. 271-322.

Morton, Eugene S. et al. Extrapair fertilizations and the evolution of colonial breeding in purple martins. *Auk,* vol. 107 no. 2, Apr. 1990, p. 273-283.

Morton, Eugene S. et al. On bluebird responses to apparent female adultery. *American Naturalist,* vol. 112, Sep./Oct. 1978, p. 968-971.

Mulder, Raoul A. and Andrew Cockburn. Sperm competition and the reproductive anatomy of male superb fairy-wrens. *Auk,* vol. 110, no. 3, Jul. 1993, p. 588-593.

Mulder, Raoul A. Faithful philanderers. *Natural History,* Nov. 1994, p. 57-62.

Myers, J.P. The Promiscuous Pectoral Sandpiper. *American Birds,* vol. 36, no. 2, Mar. 1982, p. 119-122.

Nakamura, Masahiko. Cloacal protuberance and copulatory behavior of the alpine accentor *(Prunella collaris). Auk,* vol. 107, no. 2, Apr. 1990, p. 284-295.

Negro, Juan José et al. Copulatory behaviour in a colony of lesser kestrels: sperm competition and mixed reproductive strategies. *Animal Behaviour,* vol. 43, Jun. 1992, p. 921-930.

Nelson, J. Bryan. The breeding biology of frigatebirds—a comparative review. *The Living Bird, Fourteenth Annual of the Cornell Laboratory of Ornithology,* Douglas A. Lancaster, ed., 1975, p. 113-155.

Nesbitt, Stephen A. The significance of mate loss in Florida sandhill cranes. *Wilson Bulletin,* vol. 101, no. 4, Dec. 4, 1989, p. 648-651.

Niven, Daniel K. Male-male nesting behavior in hooded warblers. *Wilson Bulletin,* vol. 105, no. 1, Mar. 1993, p. 190-193.

Noble, G.K. and Vogt, William. An experimental study of sex recognition in birds. *Auk,* vol. 52, Jul. 1935, p. 278-286.

Norris, K.J. and J.K. Blakey. Evidence for cuckoldry in the great tit *Parus major. Ibis.* Vol. 131, 1989, p. 436-442.

O'Connell, Sanjida. Macho birds sing a rousing dawn chorus. *New Scientist,* vol. 135, Sep. 5, 1992, p. 16.

Orell, Markku et al. Causes of divorce in the monogamous willow tit, *Parus montanus,* and consequences for reproductive success. *Animal Behaviour,* vol. 48, no. 5, 1994, p. 1143-1154.

Oring, Lewis W. Avian Mating systems, p. 1-79. *Avian*

Biology, Vol. VI. Donald S. Farner et al, ed. 1982.

Oring, Lewis W. and Maxson, Stephen J. Instances of simultaneous polyandry by a spotted sandpiper *Actitis macularia. Ibis,* vol. 120, 1978, p. 349-353.

Oring, Lewis W. et al. Copulation patterns and mate guarding in the sex-role reversed, polyandrous spotted sandpiper, *Actitis macularia. Animal Behaviour,* vol. 47, May 1994, p. 1065-1072.

Oring, Lewis W. et al. Cuckoldry through stored sperm in the sequentially polyandrous spotted sandpiper. *Nature,* vol. 359, Oct. 15, 1992, p. 631-633.

Peterson, Roger Tory et al. *A Field Guide to the Birds of Britain and Europe.* Houghton Mifflin Company, Boston, 1967.

Peterson, Roger Tory. *A Field Guide to the Birds.* Houghton Mifflin Company, Boston, 1980.

Peterson, Roger Tory. *A Field Guide to Western Birds.* Houghton Mifflin Company, Boston, 1990.

Petrie, Marion et al. Multiple mating in a lekking bird: why do peahens mate with more than one male and with the same male more than once? *Behavioral Ecology and Sociobiology,* vol. 31, 1992, p. 349-358.

Petrie, Marion. Mate choice in role-reversed species, p. 167-179. *Mate Choice,* Patrice Bateson, ed. Cambridge University Press, Cambridge, 1983.

Petrie, Marion. Copulation frequency in birds: why do females copulate more than once with the same male? *Animal Behaviour,* vol. 44, Oct. 1992, pl. 790-792.

Pomiankowski, Andrew. How to find the top male. *Nature,* vol. 347, Oct. 18, 1990, p. 616.

Poole, Alan. Courtship feeding and osprey reproduction. *Auk,* vol. 102, no. 3, Jul. 1985, p. 479-492.

Power, Harry W. et al. Male starlings delay incubation to avoid being cuckolded. *Auk,* vol. 98, Apr. 1981, p. 386-388.

Price, K.D. et al. Multiple parentage in broods of house wrens; genetic evidence. *Journal of Heredity,* vol. 80, 1989, p. 1-5.

Pruett-Jones, Melinda and Stephen Pruett-Jones. The bowerbird's labor of love. *Natural History,* vol. 92, no. 9, Sep. 1983, p. 48-55.

Pruett-Jones, Stephen G. and Melinda A. Pruett-Jones. Altitudinal distribution and seasonal activity patterns of birds of paradise. *National Geographic Research,* vol. 2, no. 1, Winter 1986, p. 87-105.

Prume, Richard Owen. Observations of the white-fronted manakin *(Pipra serena)* in Suriname. *Auk,* vol. 102, no. 2, Apr. 1985, p. 384-387.

Rabenold, Patricia P. et al. Shared paternity revealed by genetic analysis in cooperatively breeding tropical wrens. *Nature,* vol. 348, Dec. 6, 1990, p. 538-540.

Raloff, Janet. The gender benders. *Science News,* vol. 145, Jan. 8, 1994, p. 24-27.

Read, Andrew F. and Harvey, Paul H. Evolving in a dynamic world. *Science,* vol. 260, Jun. 18, 1993, p. 1760-1762.

Reynolds, John D. Philandering phalaropes. *Natural History,* vol 94, Aug. 1985, p. 58-65.

Ridley, Matt. Swallows and scorpionflies find symmetry is beautiful. *Science,* vol. 257, Jul. 17, 1992, p. 327-328.

Ritchison, Gary and Paul H. Klatt. Mate guarding and extra-pair paternity in northern cardinals. *Condor,* vol. 96, 1994, p. 1055-1063.

Roberts Laurel B. and William A. Searcy. Dominance relationships in harems of female red-winged blackbirds. *Auk,* vol. 105, no. 1, Jan. 1988, p. 89-96.

Rosenfield, Robert N. et al. Copulatory and other pre-incubation behaviors of Cooper's hawks. *Wilson Bulletin,* vol. 103, no. 4, Dec. 1991, p. 656-660.

Rowley, Ian. "Re-mating in birds." *Mate Choice,* ed. by Patrick Bateson. Cambridge University Press, Cambridge, 1983.

Sætre, Glenn-Peter and Tore Slagsvold. The significance of female mimicry in male contests. *American Naturalist,* vol. 147, no. 6, Jun. 1996, p. 981-995.

Sauer, E.G. Franz. Aberrant sexual behaviour in the South African ostrich. *Auk,* vol. 89, Oct., 1972, p. 717-737.

Schulze-Hagen, Karl et al. Prolonged copulation, sperm reserves and sperm competition in the aquatic warbler *Acrocephalus paludicola. Ibis,* vol. 137, Jan. 1995, p. 85-91.

Schwartz, Paul and Snow, David W. Display and related behavior of the wire-tailed manakin. *The Living Bird, Seventeenth Annual of the Cornell Laboratory of Ornithology,* Douglas A. Lancaster, ed., 1978, p. 51-78.

Scott, Dafila. Swans semper fidelis. *Natural History,* Jul. 1992, p. 26-32.

Scott, Peter. *The Swans.* Houghton Mifflin Company, Boston. 1972.

Searcy, W.A. and Yasukawa, K. Sexual selection and red-winged blackbirds. *American Scientist,* vol. 71, Mar/Apr. 1983, p. 167-174.

Seel, D.C. and K.C. Walton. Apparent polygyny in the meadow pipit. *Bird Study,* vol. 21, p. 282, 1974.

Sherman, Peter T. Social organization of cooperatively polyandrous white-winged trumpeters *(Psophia leucoptera). Auk,* vol. 112, no. 2, Apr. 1995, p. 296-309.

Shuffeldt, R.W. Polygamy and other modes of mating among birds. *American Naturalist,* vol. XLI, no. 483, Mar. 1907, p. 161-175.

Sibley, Charles G. Wren-tit attempts copulation with begging fledgling. *Condor.* vol. 54, Mar./Apr. 1952, p. 117.

Simmons, R.E. Food and the deceptive acquisition of mates by polygynous male harriers. *Behavioral Ecology and Sociobiology,* vol. 23, 1988, p. 83-92.

Simon, Hilda. *The Courtship of Birds.* Dodd, Mead & Company, New York, 1977.

Skutch, Alexander F. *Helpers at Birds' Nests.* University of Iowa Press, Iowa City, 1987.

Skutch, Alexander F. *Parent Birds and Their Young.* University of Texas Press, Austin, 1976.

Smith, James N.M. et al. Polygyny, male parental care, and sex ratio in song sparrows: an experimental study. *Auk,* vol. 99, Jul. 192, p. 555-564.

Smith, Susan M. Henpecked males and monogamy. *Journal of Field Ornithology,* vol. 51, Winter 1980, p. 56-63.

Smith, Susan M. Pair bond persistence and "divorce" in black-capped chickadees. *Wilson Bulletin,* vol. 104, no. 2, Jun. 1992, p. 338-342.

Snow, Barbara K. Guy's hermit hummingbird: visits by females, and mating. *Ibis,* vol. 116, 1974, p. 289-291.

Snow, Barbara K. Social organization of the hairy hermit: false mating. *Ardea,* vol. 61, 1973, p. 101-102.

Soler, M. and A.P. Møller. Duration of sympatry and coevolution between the great spotted cuckoo and its magpie host. *Nature,* vol. 343, Feb. 22, 1990, p. 748-750.

Sorenson, Lisa G. Forced extra-pair copulation in the white-cheeked pintail: male tactics and female responses. *Condor,* vol. 96, May 1994, p. 400-410.

Stephens, Martin L. Interspecific aggressive behavior of the polyandrous northern jacana *(Jacana spinosa). Auk,* vol. 101, no. 3, Jul. 1984, p. 508-518.

Tacha, Thomas C. Social organization of sandhill cranes from midcontinental North America. *Wildlife Monographs,* No. 99, The Wildlife Society, Inc., Oct. 1988.

Tallman, Dan A. and Richard L. Zusi. A hybrid red crossbill-pine siskin *(Loxia curvirostra x Carduelis pinus)*—and speculations on the evolution of Loxia. *Auk,* vol. 101, no. 1, Jan. 1984, p. 155-158.

Terres, John K. *The Audubon Society Encyclopedia of North American Birds.* Alfred A. Knopf, New York, 1980.

Timson, John. Nature's portable sperm bank. *New Scientist,* Apr. 2, 1994, p. 14.

Todd, Frank S. *Natural History of the Waterfowl.* Ibis Publishing Co., Vista, California, 1996.

Trainer, Jill M. and David B. McDonald. Vocal repertoire of the long-tailed manakin and its relation to male-male cooperation. *Condor,* vol. 95, no. 4, Nov. 1993, p. 769-781.

Tramer, Elliot J. and Brenda Simmers. Unusual copulatory behavior by Fiery-throated Hummingbirds. *Wilson Bulletin,* vol. 106, no. 3, Sept. 1994, p. 573-574.

Valle, Carlos A. Parental role-reversed polyandry and paternity. *Auk,* vol. 111, no. 2, Apr. 1994, p. 476-478.

Veiga, José P. Prospective infanticide and ovulation retardation in free-living house sparrows. *Animal Behaviour,* vol. 45, Jan. 1993, p. 43-46.

Veiga, José. Infanticide by male and female house sparrows. *Animal Behaviour,* vol. 39, Mar. 1990, p. 496-502.

von Haartman, Lars. Nest-site and evolution of polygamy in European passerine birds. *Ornis Fennica,* vol. 46, 1969, p. 1+

Wagner, Richard H. Evidence that female razorbills control extra-pair copulations. *Behaviour,* vol. VI, 1991, p. 157-169.

Weatherhead, Patrick J. Mixed mating strategies by females may strengthen the sexy son hypothesis. *Animal Behaviour,* vol. 47, 1994, p. 1210-1211.

West, Meredith J. and Andrew P. King. Female visual displays affect the development of male song in the cowbird. *Nature,* vol. 334, Jul. 21, 1988, p. 244-246.

Westneat, David F. and Paul W. Sherman. When monogamy isn't. *Living Bird Quarterly,* vol. 9, no. 3, Summer 1990, p. 24-28.

Westneat, David F. The relationships among polygyny, male parental care, and female breeding success in the indigo bunting. *Auk,* vol. 105, no. 2, Apr. 1988, p. 372-374.

Whittingham, Linda A. et al. Do males exchange feathers for copulations in tree swallows? *Auk,* vol. 112, Oct. 1995, p. 1079-1080.

Wilkinson, R. and T.R. Birkhead. Copulation behaviour in the vasa parrots *Coracopsis vasa and C. nigra. Ibis,* vol. 137, Jan. 1995, p. 117-119.

Wimberger, Peter H. Food supplement effects on breeding time and harem size in the red-winged blackbird *(Agelaius phoeniceus). Auk,* vol. 105, no. 4, Oct. 1988, p. 799-802.

Wingfield, John C. et al. Endocrine aspects of female-female pairing in the western Ggull *189. Animal Behaviour,* vol. 30, no. 1, Feb. 1982, p. 9-22.

Wingfield, John C. et al. Origin of homosexual pairing of female western gulls on Santa Barbara Island. p. 461-466. *The California Islands,* D.M. Power, ed., Santa Barbara Museum of Natural History, 1980.

Witmer, Mark C. Cooperative breeding by rufous hornbills on Mindanao Island, Philippines. *Auk,* vol. 110, no. 4, Oct. 1993, p. 933-936.

Wolf, Larry L. "Prostitution" behavior in a tropical hummingbird. *Condor,* vol. 77, Jul. 1975, p. 140-144.

Wright, Cathy. Bower power. *BBC Wildlife,* vol. 8, no. 11, Nov. 1990, p. 18-19.

Wyllie, Ian. The confusing cuckoo. *Birds,* vol 9, no. 6, Summer 1983, p. 36-39.

Zuñiga, Jesus M. and Tomas Redondo. No evidence for variable duration of sympatry between the great spotted cuckoo and its magpie host. *Nature,* vol. 359, Oct. 1, 1992, p. 410-411.

—Disruption is attractive. *New Scientist,* Apr. 11, 1985, p. 22

—Faithful ganders get the blues . . . *New Scientist,* vol. 114, Apr. 9, 1987, p. 27.

—Murder in the barn. *Science 85,* Dec. 1985, p. 8.

—Oystercatcher's divorce. *New Scientist,* vol. 113, Feb. 5, 1987, p. 43.